SIMPLY

MERTON

Wisdom from His Journals

LINUS MUNDY

Franciscan
MEDIA
Cincinnati, Ohio

Cover and book design by Mark Sullivan

Cover image © Bob Baker

LIBRARY OF CONGRESS CATALOGING-IN-PUBLICATION DATA

Mundy, Linus.

Simply Merton : wisdom from his journals / Linus Mundy.

pages cm

Includes bibliographical references.

ISBN 978-1-61636-763-3

1. Merton, Thomas, 1915-1968. 2. Merton, Thomas, 1915-1968—Quotations. I. Title.

BX4705.M542M86 2014

271'.12502—dc23

2014016175

ISBN 978-1-61636-763-3

Published by Franciscan Media

28 W. Liberty St.

Cincinnati, OH 45202

www.FranciscanMedia.org

Printed in the United States of America.

Printed on acid-free paper.

14 15 16 17 18 5 4 3 2 1

Dedicated, with much love and gratitude, to:
FR. MATTHEW KELTY, O.C.S.O.

THE MONKS OF THE ABBEY OF GETHSEMANI,
Trappist, Kentucky

THE SISTERS OF ST. BENEDICT,
Monastery Immaculate Conception,
Ferdinand, Indiana

THE MONKS OF SAINT MEINRAD ARCHABBEY,
St. Meinrad, Indiana

THE FRANCISCAN FRIARS OF
ST. JOHN THE BAPTIST PROVINCE,
Cincinnati, Ohio

THE SISTERS OF PROVIDENCE,
St. Mary-of-the-Woods, Indiana

CONTENTS

✳

The voice of Thomas Merton is alive and with us still. This book tries to capture the essence of Thomas Merton—what really mattered to him during his life (1915–1968). But just as much, this book is about how these same important themes that Merton cared about still matter to us, one hundred years after his birth.

The commentary and reflections in this book relate to Merton's life and works, especially concentrating on his journals. It is in our journals that we are perhaps most honest. And although Merton had the courage to be honest and forthright all his life, we see the honesty and directness shining through in these selections.

In some of the earlier biographies of Merton, there were references to his "restricted journals." These are now all in print and have been devoured—all 1.3 million words—by Merton aficionados like myself. And in my opinion at least, his journals contain some of Merton's very best thinking and writing.

(I am also a huge admirer of the recorded talks Merton gave to Gethsemani novices in the early 1960s. Here we not only hear his real voice but also pick up his wit and humor and enthusiasm.)

As to the Merton journals, it is wise to remember that when one journals privately, one journals freely and without censorship or perhaps even self-censorship. Self-expression and candor are important in the journaling process. And so the "journalist" may very well exaggerate certain points in order to let off steam—or perhaps just to run certain ideas up the flagpole and see how they look or sound.

So I would caution not to read too much into any single quotation or comment—especially when it is Thomas Merton who is doing the writing! He could be very, very sure of himself, but he also had a noteworthy penchant for rethinking issues, changing his mind, adding important postscripts—all the while admitting openly that by the time he has written something it may no longer be totally what he meant to say or where he stood now on the issue.

In order to give, in my view, a fuller picture of Merton's beliefs then, I draw here and there from the complete Merton literary canon. I take pride in having read as much as possible all the words that Merton himself penned, and have made an effort here to put forth what I consider his seminal thoughts and ideas on each of fifteen key themes. The themes chosen are the ones I deemed most important in his life and works—themes of perennial value, some of which were rather visionary indeed for Merton's own time.

About Merton: Some years ago noted Irish writer Malachy McCourt wrote a book titled *A Monk Swimming*. It was a play on McCourt's childhood misunderstanding of the words from the Hail Mary: "Blessed art thou, a monk swimming." This present work might alternatively be entitled *Thomas Merton: A Monk Swimming*, with chapters such as "A Monk Swimming Alone," "A Monk Swimming in Troubled Waters," "A Monk Swimming Against the Current." For these were the experiences of Thomas Merton as monk and writer, prophet and priest, seeker and searcher, hermit and celebrity.

I remember when I heard the tragic news that Thomas Merton had died. I was just a couple of years out of a five-year stint at a Catholic seminary. In the seminary much was made of the writing of this young monk, and I was an avid fan as well. But it was 1968 and I was now a seminary drop-out, and was attending a big (and eye-opening!) state university. The passage from seminary to a state university in the 1960s was dramatic indeed, and perhaps not unlike the contrast between Merton's early life and his arrival at Gethsemani—only perhaps in reverse.

The truth is that while his twenty-six years of living as a monk might seem to have been a fixed life, it was anything but that: Merton's mind and heart were constantly on the move. He was "swimming" indeed, both above and below the surface. And the only real constant was his desire to please God.

In the excellent book *Merton by Those Who Knew Him Best*, Rembert Weakland, O.S.B., sums up the life of this "swimming monk," if you will: "Merton, to me, was a great searcher. He was constantly unhappy, as all great searchers are. He was constantly ill at ease, he was constantly restless, as all searchers are—because that's part of the search. And in that sense he was the perfect monk. Contemplation isn't satisfaction—it's search."

It is this searching, wandering, wondering Merton that appeals to so many of us today. We see ourselves in him; we see ourselves and our deepest yearnings and wonderings in the topics he wrote and talked and obsessed about.

This book attempts to single out some of the very themes Merton spent his days and nights praying over, writing about, pondering. The book, if anything, will show the purity of his intentions, his commitment to seeking God and finding truth. We will also see the purity of his loneliness and longing for this truth. It is impossible to include more than a fraction of what he left for us in his writings, not to mention his talks and conversations. (His journals alone, as we have said, contain well over one million words.)

But there are recurring themes in the life of Merton, and many are certainly enduring. Some are nothing less than prophetic and visionary. These are topics that still matter to us, and perhaps more than ever, as we modern-day seekers share an ultimate sentiment with Thomas Merton: He may have been confused, frustrated, yearning, restless, searching—and we will explore some of these experiences, including experiences of sheer recklessness on his part. But all the while, and in the final analysis, we will find a Thomas Merton who valued what was true above what was expedient or fashionable. And we will see a Merton who was profoundly courageous, although he was quoted as saying, "Courage comes and goes. Hold on for the next supply."

Through it all, he proved to be as courageous and tough as he needed to be in never ceasing his search for the Divine. He could conclude with the greatest certainty that in all his work and life: "I am happy that I can at least want to love God."

How I Came to Know Merton

I have a friend who calls me "The Gethseminator." I don't mind that. As a matter of fact, he could even call me a "Mertinator" and I would be happy about that, too. You'll see traces of my enthusiasm for Merton throughout this book, no doubt. I can't hide it. There are a great many of us enthusiasts out there—and you yourself may be one also.

When I first started going to Gethsemani on retreats more than thirty years ago, the term for people like me was "monk-happy." Monk-happy people are those who know that monks know something deep-down that the rest of us are still trying to learn. Monks, as my friend Fr. Matthew Kelty put it so well in one of the first sermons I heard him preach at Gethsemani, are folks "who are not freeloaders. There is no beauty without the harsh dedication to the common, to the love of Jesus with one another and for a dying world that so needs the witness of men who believe what they say." We monks, he went on, "know where we are going and we know how to get there. And honey, we are on our way."

At the end of his usual after-Compline talk that night, I told Kelty how moved I was by his sermon that day. An hour or so later I heard the whisper of sheets of paper sliding under my guest room door. Kelty had made a copy of his sermon and put a note on it for me: "A souvenir of your visit to Gethsemani. Love to you. Matthew."

Kelty and I kept up a modest correspondence over the following decades, and we spoke often when I was on retreat at Gethsemani. Once in a letter to me he responded to my quote from writer Annie Dillard that, "The impulse to keep to yourself what you have learned is not only shameful, it is destructive. Anything you do not give freely and abundantly becomes lost to you. You open your safe and find ashes." Continued Kelty,

"Odd, one time I asked Merton why he wrote *everything* down. His journals were just a part of that. His answer: 'If you don't, it is lost.' So the two agree."

And if you are blessed enough to witness monks in action (or is it inaction?) enough, you come to see extraordinary individual monks who agree on the essence of their lives. They really "get it." Matthew Kelty got it. Thomas Merton got it in spades. He was the consummate monk, most would say, despite his transgressions that had come to be publicly known. Indeed, he perhaps worked harder at his monastic profession because of his desire to make personal conversion an everyday concern.

In the decades since his tragic death in 1968, writers have come forth with excellent books about Merton's life, thought, practice, and teachings. Most writers, like myself, are tempted to sum up Merton's life and works in just a few words. For example, it would not be inaccurate to state simply that "Merton's life was dedicated to God alone."

"God alone" has indeed become a sort of Trappist (as well as Carthusian) mantra over the years, and Merton took the phrase particularly seriously. He also came to object to any simplistic translations of the phrase, as we will see in one of the chapters of this book. And yet his own interpretation of this phrase would run to thousands and thousands of pages of books, articles, letters, and journals over his adult life. It was not just two simple words.

There are those who would say, and I think Merton himself would be included, that his life could never be boiled down two words, or two thousand, or two million. Merton, however, would become annoyed when he heard people describe him as a spiritual giant, a person with special insights, one possessing rare and secret gifts, or one who had ventured out into a life of spiritual experimentation. At one point he reached the point of exasperation, and wrote, partly tongue-in-cheek:

> This is not a hermitage—it is a house.... What I wear is pants. What I do is live. How I pray is breathe. Who said Zen? Wash out your mouth if you said Zen. If you see a meditation going by, shoot it.... The spiritual life is something that people worry about when they are so busy with something else they think they ought to be doing.

This book, then, neither tries to sell short the deep-down, simple Merton nor his wondrous complexity. By calling this work *Simply Merton*, the intent is rather to offer a work that is an essential Merton, a genuine Merton, a book that is all Merton. And to me that means a book that is all you and me, dear reader—all of us very human beings, yet beings profoundly anointed by the Divine. Some would say that it was Merton's tragic distinction to have suffered his agony for all of us. Indeed, it is idle to speak of Merton's defects as it is exactly these defects that we find so ingratiating, so like our own.

One other reason I am writing this book is that Merton and I have some things in common (well, *some* things, such as when he writes, in 1966: "There is an immense amount of nonsense in me.") But I have made note of some commonalities over the years: In 1915, my dad and Thomas Merton were born only a week apart from each other; Merton and I—just like perhaps many thousands of others—share the same Enneagram personality profile, as well as the same Myers-Briggs personality profile, and we both hold bachelor's and master's degrees in English.

But a bit more specifically, Merton and I were both living under the roof of an abbey at the same time in the 1960s. He was living under far more challenging conditions, in one of the strictest of the strict monasteries. Additionally, he had taken solemn vows; I was discerning my own vocation.

I was living in a strict seminary under the tutelage and watchful eye of a community of Benedictine monks, some of whom thought they were running a boot camp. At least that's how we seminarians looked at it. There was plenty of austerity and deprivation: We slept in large, open dormitory rooms, rooms with as many as forty bunk beds in each. That's eighty young boys. We were required to observe, with the monks, The Great Silence which began at 9 P.M. and did not end until breakfast, which was after our 5:55 A.M. rising, followed by Mass. Certain monks were assigned as disciplinarians, who strolled the dorms, and so on, for violators.

I would exaggerate if I were to say it was all out of one of those great Dickens—if not Victor Hugo—novels. (It is probably not an exaggeration at all for Merton). Deprivation, austerity, all nonessentials stripped away—but all easily worth it since it was for a higher purpose. And, besides—at least for me—the home I had left in order to attend seminary had its own Dickensian features.

At seminary, most of our meals were taken in silence, or there was a selection of inspirational table reading (sometimes something from Thomas Merton). We were permitted to leave the seminary only for Christmas and summer vacation, with visitors allowed one day per month.

By contrast, however, I suspect that candidates and monks of Gethsemani at the time would have examined our Saint Meinrad regimen and called it tame, undemanding, perhaps even cushy. After all, Cistercians were founded on the notion that the Benedictines were good and all, but there needed to be a branch of it that ratcheted things up a few notches.

I did have an older cousin who ratcheted things up a bit out there in the country near the Saint Meinrad abbey. His name was Fr. Prosper Lindauer, O.S.B., and he also happened to be one of my teachers in seminary. He received permission at midlife to live the rest of his days as a hermit out on the monastery grounds.

Fr. Prosper was a bit eccentric, perhaps, but a very holy eccentric. He had become something of a gourmet cook, dishing up exotic vegetarian dishes, and amazing bread loaves, for an occasional visitor. (He would return to the Saint Meinrad abbey for books, supplies, medical care, etc.). I recall on one occasion checking out a book from the abbey library called *Wild Animals at My Door.* Those were the days when there was a library card in the back of every book. The only name on the card—the only person who had checked out this book before I did—was Fr. Prosper, the hermit. Does this also help qualify me to write a book about a hermit? OK, I may be stretching things.

But Thomas Merton and Prosper Lindauer were kindred spirits; I can relate to these guys. But then again, so can millions of others. He, like so many of us, traveled a long path to self-understanding, a path that can seem endless. But Merton, like few others, gives us this idea that it is OK to travel the long path, to take the long way home, to be confused, quirky, a doubter, even a sinner (to a point). He gives us permission to have no idea where we are going, or to be a sinner and one seeking to be back on the track to holiness at the same time. He leads us to believe that maybe we are better than we think we are—if we want to be better.

A Brief Merton Biography

Thomas Merton was born in 1915 in France. His mother was American and his father a New Zealander. He was educated in

France, and then studied at Cambridge. There he had a rather rakish social life, drinking, partying, eventually fathering a child (of whom it is said died, with the child's mother, in the blitz of London in WWII). He then went on to Columbia University in New York, where he was deeply affected by reading Étienne Gilson's *The Spirit of Medieval Philosophy*. He decided to become a Catholic.

After his application to become a Franciscan was rejected, he eventually joined the Trappists (Order of Cistercians of the Strict Observance), at Our Lady of Gethsemani, in Kentucky. It was a religious order, and a monastery, that had an established reputation as one that was the strictest of the strict. The official date was December 13, 1941. In 1948, his autobiography, a modern conversion story, *The Seven Storey Mountain*, was published, and became an international bestseller. This book was followed by such revered classics as *Seeds of Contemplation, Waters of Siloe, The Ascent to Truth*, and *New Seeds of Contemplation*. He went on to write numerous books, articles, poetry, and voluminous letters and extensive journals for the rest of his life.

Says Ursula King in her book *Christian Mystics*,

> Merton is one of the most influential contempo-
> rary spiritual writers. Few in our time have spoken
> so inspiringly of the 'deep movements of love' that
> come in the highest reaches of contemplation. His

writings reveal a deep familiarity with the tradition of Catholic mystical theology, but he also came under the influence of Eastern mysticism, particularly that of Zen Buddhism. In 1968 he traveled to the East, met with the Dalai Lama, and participated in a monastic renewal conference in Bangkok, where he died through an accident. He was electrocuted coming out of the shower in his bedroom, apparently slipping and grabbing onto a large, stand-up fan with faulty wiring.

For many years at the monastery, Merton longed to live as a hermit, and only a few years before his death was granted permission to do so, living in a simple cinder block building on a hill near the monastery. There he took most of his meals, prayed, worked, and slept in solitude. He continued sharing in the liturgical life of the monastic community, attending services there, and also participating in the formation of novices, as well as pursuing his ecumenical and interreligious ministry. Concludes Ursula King, "Merton was like a hermit 'living with wisdom' in the modern world. He left an extraordinary spiritual legacy…and quite a number of groups have come into existence devoted to the study of his thought and spiritual practice."

What people have said about Thomas Merton:

You looked into his eyes and there were "deeps" there.
—Fellow monk Matthew Kelty, O.C.S.O.,
to the author, 1985

I think that Thomas Merton could easily be called the greatest spiritual writer and spiritual master of the twentieth century in English speaking America.
—Jonathan Montaldo

There is no other person who has such a profound influence on those writing on spiritual topics, not only on Catholics, but non-Catholics, as Merton has.
—Lawrence Cunningham

What's so shocking is that Merton kept breaking new ground. He became the first Catholic priest in U.S. history to denounce nuclear weapons and war and racism, and he studied Mahatma Gandhi and the Chinese mystics and Zen Buddhism when people had never heard of Zen or Buddhism. He was not only bringing cultures together, he was bringing the different religions together, and all the while going deep into the common ground of all of the religions, which is the wisdom of nonviolence. Recently one of the biggest Catholic theologians in the United States, David Tracy, said, 'Where will the Church be two hundred years from now?' And he answered his own question without missing a beat: "We're all going to be trying to catch up to Thomas Merton. He's gone ahead of everybody.' That's how significant a historical figure Merton now is, not just in the American Church, but maybe in the history of the church."

—John Dear, S.S.

I want to see him as someone who's very much like all of us. If you want to call him a saint, that's fine, but what does it mean? He's a person who struggled to do the will of God, who realized his faults. His clay feet are there for all of us to see. He certainly would not want any kind of adulation given to him in the way of sainthood. He once had a letter from a young man who said that he wanted to become his disciple, and Merton wrote back and said, "Don't try to be. I don't have disciples. I don't want any disciples. Don't build your life on a mud pile like me. Be a disciple of Jesus Christ."

—Jonathan Montaldo

Note

Of all the biographies of Thomas Merton, I would most recommend *The Seven Mountains of Thomas Merton*, by Michael Mott, published in 1984 by Houghton Mifflin, Boston. This one is the most detailed and written in an objective and honest tone, after an enormous amount of research. It is also extremely readable.

Serious students of Merton know that the vast majority of primary source matter and archival Merton material is housed at The Thomas Merton Center, Bellarmine University, Louisville, Kentucky. The Center contains more than 50,000 items, including the literary estate, 15,000 pieces of correspondence to over 2,100 individuals, 900 drawings by Merton, 1,100 photographs, and 600 hours of audio conferences given by Thomas Merton.

CHAPTER ONE

Simplicity

I truly seek a very solitary, simple and primitive life with no labels attached.

However, there must be love in it, and not an abstract love but a real love for real people.

Why did Thomas Merton come to the Abbey of Gethsemani and become a Trappist monk? A simple answer is: to live simply. That is what Gethsemani stood for. (Albeit one writer described the place as "a kind of training ground for death.")

There is a sign—an old historic marker—just as one enters the grounds of the abbey. It was there even before the young Merton first came to visit. The few words on the sign tell just what Trappists do: "They are noted for their prayer, labor, and silence." Although, when frustrated, Merton once blurted out that none of the monks really knew why they were there, he did know in his heart why he and his brothers came there: to live the simple life, focusing on God alone—in their prayer, in their labor, and in their silence.

The great irony is that his life turned out to be anything but simple, even while it always remained firmly grounded in one purpose alone: to strip away all that was distracting, all that was excessive or complicated or false. This is the same reason so many of us pilgrims, myself included, journey to that old abbey in central Kentucky again and again.

In my more than thirty years of retreating at Gethsemani, I see my fellow retreatants—not to mention the monks themselves—daily tossing off, as Merton did, the things of the world that are too complex, too cumbersome, too taxing. Merton had lived the bright-lights-big-city life and had found it wanting; he found it soul-draining. He was ready to trade in his high-speed New York City taxicabs and subways for a one-speed bike. Actually, make that a walking stick.

His goal was to become carefree. "All I want," he wrote in his journal on August 28, 1941, quoting St. Anselm, "is to retreat a little from my daily concerns. This is the thing I want to do. To enter into the cell of the mind and exclude all but God." And then, twenty-four years later (January 31, 1965), upon becoming a hermit: "But what more do I seek than this silence, this simplicity...? For me, there is nothing else...and to think that I have had the grace to taste a little of what all men seek without realizing it!"

I share one of my own brief journal entries while on retreat at Gethsemani over twenty-five years ago. It was for me a time that I was in a particularly feverish mood to "get down to business" and shed the troubling nonessentials in my life:

> September 23, 1988—Gethsemani: Just checked into room 207 and *boom*, a powerful thunderstorm! Ahh, Gethsemani—one of the sweetest places on earth. Sweet? Well…peaceful. God-full. Rain pouring down my open window onto the courtyard. I already feel the Gethsemani rain washing away layer upon layer of my caked-on, baked-on disguises. First goes the "rich" business, and then all that "famous" business I've dreamt of, and then the idea of being a great rescuer of all distressed persons in the world. And what is left?! Well, it's still raining. But we're now down to a guy who has vowed just a few moments ago to try to do two simple things with the rest of my life: 1) love God; 2) love people.

The Abbey of Gethsemani had that kind of effect on people in 1988, as it did in 1941 when Merton came to the place he called "The center of America." It was—and remains today—a place to be free…a place to come to and do "nothing" but spend one's time simply for and with God. And Merton did this simple living the entire second half of his fifty-three-year life, both as a monk in community and then in his last years as a hermit in the Gethsemani woods.

Life was indeed simple at Gethsemani in the 1940s when Merton entered the monastery, and Merton had heard much about the place. Its reputation was one that would put a scare into many. Indeed, hearsay had it that the monks slept in their coffins and prayed continually for death. It was unquestionably a place for living a hard-scrabble life of prayer and penance.

But Merton was more than ready and willing to dive right in to this kind of life—if it led to holiness, if it led to God. And so it was that he lived a life where the monks slept on straw pallets on boards; their cells were small canvas-walled cubicles. They fasted most of the time and ate primarily bread and vegetables. The farm work in the Kentucky summer could be merciless, and was interrupted only by the *Ordo*, the Liturgy of the Hours, the nine times a day worship services beginning at 3:15 A.M. in the abbey church choir, half the monks on one side, half on the other. The winters were the toughest, however, and biographer Mott says that it was the cold that the monks at Gethsemani remembered most, the days in central Kentucky when the holy water froze in the fonts.

One of the rules of the Order was silence—albeit a rather sophisticated sign language took its place now and then. Behind all of this poverty, there was chastity and obedience to the abbot, until death.

When Merton finally was given permission to live in the hermitage full-time (before that it was for designated periods only), some of the rules had changed, but not the most basic ones. It was still to be a life of penance and prayer.

It was one of Merton's contemporaries in the monastery, Fr. Matthew Kelty, who years ago gave me a personal tour of Merton's hermitage, remarking that he himself helped Merton "pick out the curtains," and also related how "Merton's life here was hard."

Kelty was a brilliant poet and beautiful, cheery-eyed holy man who had himself been both a monk and then a monk-hermit, in Papua, New Guinea. He had summed up that life in a somewhat tongue-in-cheek way in his book *Flute Solo*: "I mean I am really doing nothing…it seems a strange role…. To come down to it, the monk does 'nothing.' Though I must say that when there are one hundred of them doing it, it is a bit more impressive." For myself, I was impressed that he as a hermit would ride a motorcycle up and down the beaches of Papua New Guinea, and then occasionally hop off of it to stroll/dance by the waterside playing his flute.

But Merton did not come to Gethsemani to do nothing; he wanted to renounce, to strip away, all that was not God. And Gethsemani was probably the one best monastery in America with a five-star rating for austerity and discipline and personal sacrifice for God's sake alone.

As Merton wrote in his journal dated February 14, 1948: "The greatest joy is to give up yourself altogether for the honor and glory of God, to know you belong to him entirely,… Anything that tends to that end, any sacrifice, therefore, brings joy and happiness, even though it may be bitter to the flesh." This notion of making a sacrifice was surely for Merton tied in to the larger notion of "making up" for his past sins, fleeing to a *refugium peccatorum*—a refuge of sinners—where things could be made right through the proper penances and sacrifices. Gethsemani was what Merton was looking for. It was a place where the slate was wiped clean for him.

The utter simplicity Merton sought demanded many self-sacrifices. He was ready to lose his life, the life the world told him he should have. He had become convinced instead that, as T.S. Eliot says in *Little Gidding*, "the one great purpose in life must cost not less than everything."

One of the things this life did not take from him, however—but rather gave to him by way of paradox—was a new sense of freedom. It was both a freedom *from,* and a freedom *for.* Merton wrote much about this liberation especially when in the "prison" (of all places) of his hermitage. Like the earliest of monastics, the desert mystics of the fourth and fifth centuries, Merton was in this new and desolate place finally free to confront not only himself fiercely and fully, but also to confront God on a most intimate level.

He was following the dramatic voice of Tolstoy writing in his short story, "Life Is a Lie": "No. No lie," Tolstoy concludes.

"Renounce *for* something, not *against*." Merton was, more than anything, renouncing *for* something. It was a life of simplicity—of simple abundance—where he could be spiritually free and full of God alone.

Merton on Simplicity

It is terrible to want to belong entirely to God, and see nothing around you but the world and not see him. In the monastery you don't see him either but you have nothing to do but lament your separation from him and pray to him, and pray for the world. In the world itself, your prayers are drowned by the noise of traffic: you have to watch out for cars, falling buildings, brimstone, thunder.

This is the center of America.... This is the only real city in America—in a desert.

Give up everything for God. You say that, and you don't know what you mean.

My beautiful dream about a silent, solitary, well ordered life of perfect contemplation and perfect monastic observance, with no intrusion from the world, no publicity, no best-selling books, just God and that nice archaic little Carthusian cell!!

Afternoons are for nothing. For cutting away all that is practical. Learn to wash your cup and give rise to nothing. What house? No house could possibly make a difference. It is a house for nothing. It has no purpose. Do not give it one, and the whole universe will be thankful.

In the morning I heard a truck coming up through the fields…the sink and cabinet were arriving (I still use the outhouse, however; no indoor toilet). So my kitchen was finally fixed up, the water connected… and I don't have to wash the dishes in a bucket on the floor….To celebrate I had a supper of chop-suey and rice, and walked in the clear cool evening utterly at peace and happy….

Finding Simplicity in Our Lives

I went to the Abbey of Gethsemani for a retreat for the first time in 1981. I was running late. I quickly checked into my simple room, took a glance at a single bed that was about two-thirds the width and four times the hardness of a standard single bed. Then I hustled to the dining room for supper. There were only a couple of guys in line in front of me as we were putting the food onto our trays. Gosh, I thought, looking at the food offerings: All of the main dish entrées were gone; nothing but boiled onion was left. Well, you guessed it: The boiled onion *was* the main dish! Talk about simplicity.

SIMPLICITY

For Reflection

Can we become "rockets"? Here I share an entry from my
journal, written at Gethsemani on October 17, 1993:

> Listened at breakfast to an audiotape observing the
> tenth anniversary of Merton's death. The tape closed
> with the ending of *The Seven Story Mountain*, that
> hard ending that says it doesn't matter and you don't
> know and that it all matters and God knows: You're
> going to suffer, friend, if you wanna live right. It has
> to be. God's gonna getcha and it's gonna hurt before it
> doesn't and before all's well, very well, very, very well.
> Also in that tape is a comment by Dom Flavian
> Burns, one of Merton's abbots, who says something
> like: "Down here we can become rockets. At our best,
> when we're what we're supposed to be, we're rockets.
> Everything is stripped away but what's rocket. Not the
> slightest bit of extra weight or decoration or cargo. So
> we either soar—like a rocket. Or we don't, which is
> the greatest tragedy—because rockets soar. Period. Or
> they're not rockets." Yeah, I like that. And I don't think
> it's just for Merton and the monks by a long shot.

To be a bit preachy: We in the modern world have this idea
of happiness that, some would say, borders on sinfulness or
something approaching sin. The way our culture tells us to

9

find happiness is to do and believe things that actually become obstacles to our salvation.

It takes a lot of courage to step out of what may seem like a "forced march" and concentrate on both our physical and spiritual lives. It takes courage to do things differently than our neighbors and friends are doing them. Merton, however, one time said it this way: "Courage comes and goes. Hold on for the next supply.

CHAPTER TWO

Becoming One's True Self

This is my life and I don't pretend to understand it.

"Always we begin again" is a motto of Benedictine monks. Actually it is more than a motto; it is one of the vows they take—the vow of *conversatio,* or constant conversion. The Trappists, the Order of Cistercians of the Strict Observance (O.C.S.O.), are a branch of Benedictines.

For most Benedictines and all of us who want to apply wholesome Benedictine values to our lives, "Always we begin again" simply and wonderfully means we can fall down and get up; we can sin and start over; we can make terrible mistakes and be forgiven. For Merton, "Always we begin again" also seemed to mean there could be no end to the questioning, the restlessness, the discerning about what is next, what is right, what is true.

Interestingly, I think, for those of us who keep journals—I have been doing so since 1967—these journals tend to fill up with entries on recurring themes. Over the years there are constant "replays" of previous questions, previous scenes. Things—especially deep down things—don't seem to change for us over the years.

In his own journals, Merton often makes such statements as: "OK, now I have it"; "Finally I have the answer"; "It is now crystal clear to me"; "Once and for all I have come to an understanding"; "This is it!" It is as though we human beings believe we have to keep weighing every decision and question. Or maybe we fall back on Emerson's conclusion that "A foolish consistency is the hobgoblin of little minds."

And so, most of us keep up the search for the end of the rainbow, for El Dorado, the pot of gold, nirvana, God, our true selves. Why? Because, as St. Catherine of Siena knew, "If you are what you should be, you will set the whole world ablaze."

In my view there were two major character traits that made it so tough for Merton to find inner peace, to discern the right way to live. First, Merton's biggest nemesis was his idealism. He wanted to be the perfect monk; he strove to be the perfect Christian. Second, Merton's talents and interests allowed him to be so many things—and he was good at all of them. Merton was a scholar, a researcher, a teacher, an intellectual, an artist, a writer, and a monk. His interests were deep and wide: jazz, French literature, poetry, Church history, the saints, patristics, liturgy, contemplation, theology, Eastern religions and philosophy, Western philosophy, monasticism, sociology. He had a deep love of learning and an unquenchable thirst for knowledge, especially of all things spiritual.

At Columbia University in 1939, at age twenty-four, he is quoted to have stated flatly, "My chief concern was now to see myself in print." Although Merton was known as something of a ladies' man, albeit a sometimes shy one, his biographer Michael Mott says that Merton's friends at Columbia described him as much more obsessed with being a writer than with pursuing women.

"Writer" seemed to be the right fit, the right "self" to wear at that time. It was only two years later, however, in 1941, that he was officially accepted into the monastic order of Trappists, the Order of Cistercians of the Strict Observance. And as a fervent young monk he was willing to offer up even this very "self" he cared so much about—his self as a writer. Fortunately, for him and for all of us, this offer was not accepted by his abbot. The abbot instead encouraged Merton to be both monk and writer, believing he could help the community and the Church in both of these professions.

Not long before his entry to Gethsemani, Merton felt he was truly on the very verge of getting to a place—physically, mentally, spiritually—where he could become himself:

And there will be no more future—not in the world, not in geography, not in travel, not in change, not in variety, conversations, new york, new problem in writing, new friends, none of that: but a far better progress, all interior and quiet!!! If God would only grant it! If it were only His will.

Once he became a member of the Gethsemani community, Merton's ongoing efforts to become his true self were from then on centered primarily on what was the best definition of "monk" and monastic life; what was the best environment for living the life of a monk-writer to the full; what were the themes and topics that were most suitable for his vocation as a monk-writer; in what ways he could become more and more united with God. We will treat these various topics in the chapters that follow.

We will also touch on one very dramatic test he was subjected to in his mid-life years: He had fallen head over heels for a nurse in Louisville, while he was a patient in a hospital there in the mid-1960s. Merton was, as it were, testing the radical philosophy of St. Augustine who daringly stated: "Love and do what you will." This was 1966. It was the year I left the seminary and probably a record year for seminary dropouts in general. Like Merton that year, we wanted to test some things "out there" in the world. It was probably the worst year of my life. Merton, looking back at the amorous events of that year, made a similar conclusion, referring to the whole affair as some "foolishness."

My own reading of this is, Merton's love affair was stupid, embarrassing, reckless, crazy, desperate, blind, wrong, foolish— and understandable. He knew that love of others, love of another, are all part of the human milieu, and in this case the human dilemma. Many of the lyrics in the songs of that time, such as Jefferson Airplane's "Somebody to Love" or Bob Dylan's "Blowin' in the Wind," had more than an inkling of permission in them to do one's own thing, to be free. (Merton comments on Dylan several times in his journals, one time admitting that he'd really like to meet this guy. He did meet Dylan's folk-singer friend Joan Baez as she and a friend shared some drinks and conversation on the Gethsemani grounds.)

In 1967, *Day of a Stranger* appeared in print. In it Merton quotes from one of his own middle-of-the-night reflections on love and companionship and intimacy:

> One might say I had decided to marry the silence of the forest. The sweet dark warmth of the whole world will have to be my wife. Out of the heart of that dark warmth comes the secret that is heard only in silence, but is the root of all the secrets that are whispered by all lovers in their beds all over the world. So perhaps I have an obligation to preserve the stillness, the silence,

the poverty, the virginal point of pure nothingness which is at the center of all other loves. I attempt to cultivate this plant without comment in the middle of the night and water it with psalms and prophecies in silence. It becomes the most rare of all the trees in the garden, at once the primordial paradise tree, the *axis mundi*, the cosmic axle and the Cross. *Nulla silva talem profert.* There is only one such tree. It cannot be multiplied. It is not interesting.

The 1960s were a troubled, confusing time, to say the least. We were all trying to find ourselves. Many, many folks felt, like Merton did, that they were "ducks in a chicken coop." At one point in 1966, Merton comes out and says to a friend that he likes people, "but after about an hour" he is tired of being with others. Just a couple of years before that decade of the 1960s, one gets a great insight into Merton's mixed-up feelings about his place in this changing world. Merton was seeing a psychologist who was trying to help him find himself. To Merton's annoyance, the psychologist concludes that, "You want a hermitage in Times Square with a large sign over it saying 'HERMIT.'"

Merton on Becoming One's True Self

Trees and animals have no problem. God makes them what they are without consulting them, and they are perfectly satisfied. With us it is different. God leaves us free to be whatever we like. We can be ourselves or not, as we please.

How do you expect to reach your own perfection by leading someone else's life? His sanctity will never be yours; you must have the humility to work out your own salvation in a darkness where you are absolutely alone.

Many poets are not poets for the same reason that many religious men are not saints: they never succeed in being themselves. They never get around to being the particular poet or the particular monk they are intended to be by God. They never become the man or the artist who is called for by all the circumstances of their individual lives.

If we are called to the place in which God wills to do us the most good, it means we are called where we can best leave ourselves and find Him. The mercy of God demands to be known and recognized and set apart from everything else and praised and adored in joy. Every vocation is, therefore, at once a vocation to sacrifice and to joy. It is a call to the knowledge of God, to the recognition of God as our Father, to joy in the understanding of His mercy.

Becoming One's True Self in Our Lives

Gethsemani has always been a very important place of discernment for me. I have gone there many times with a heavy agenda on my mind, decisions to make, amends to make, deliberations with results that would affect my family, my coworkers, and on and on. This is an entry from my journal from August 18, 1986, a few weeks before a scheduled retreat at Gethsemani:

> I am reading Thomas Greene, S.J.'s book, *A Vacation with the Lord*. Greene says that when Jesus came out of the Garden, he left with a crisis resolved. He had said "Yes" to the Father, and that "Yes" was forever. I too have gone to the garden, and come back with crises resolved. I'm going again next month.

One of the big discernment issues for all of us, as it was with Thomas Merton, is to figure out just who and what we are. How can we differentiate between our true and false selves? To be like Jesus, we need to be honest with ourselves. Who, really, are we? And what has God created us (me) to be? It can be a long and painful process figuring out this reality. After all, we have become very adroit at naming our own reality, faults and all, sometimes totally blind to our very selves.

The key, then, is to yield to the self that you are—to the plan that God is unfolding in your heart, even though you may be feeling disconnected from that heart at the moment.

For Reflection

An interesting discernment exercise to examine who you are might be to draw up two lists. First, make a list of words that describe who and what you are, for example: *honest, kind, confused, idealistic, tired, worried, satisfied, lonely, wealthy, competent, driven, humble.*

Next, make a second list, using the words to describe yourself after you have become the true self you want to be, the true self God wants you to be.

Finally, make a short list of single words that describe in very practical terms exactly what you will need to do (or not do) to become this true self.

CHAPTER THREE

Conversion

"Give up everything for God...." You say that, and
you don't know what you mean.

[The next day:] A contemplative is not one who lives
for contemplation, but one who lives for God alone.

One of the greatest Christian conversion stories is that of St.
Paul, who received his wake-up call from none other than the
resurrected Christ. Saul, later Paul, was knocked off his donkey
and accusingly questioned by Christ, "Saul, Saul, why do you
persecute me?" Merton could have related to the Paul conversion story, as anyone with a heightened conscience might.

But another powerful religious conversion story might
make for a better comparison to the conversion and subse-
quent life of Thomas Merton. I refer to the tale in Herman
Hesse's *Siddhartha*. It is, to me, strikingly similar to the Merton
conversion story, especially as we examine Merton's ongoing
conversion.

Siddhartha tells of a young man who wants to cure his "sickness with life" by immersing himself in sacred teaching and live as a semi-recluse. One critic of this classic book says the power in the work is in the contrast displayed: "the restless departures and the search for stillness at home; the diversity of experience and the harmony of a unifying spirit; the security of religious dogma and the anxiety of freedom." This may well be young Siddhartha's story, but I myself have never seen a better summary of the life of Thomas Merton in his great "seeking" years.

Merton was ready for a change, as he tells us in his own autobiography, *The Seven Storey Mountain*. Here he tells the dramatic truth of his younger days, from his birth in 1915 until his fifth year of living as a Trappist monk. But his very life and actions in almost all of his monastic years tell of his struggle for ongoing conversion: his search to cure his own "sickness with life," like Siddhartha; his "restless departures" at least in mind and spirit if not in body, where he kept looking for change, for something newer and better not only for himself but for God; his "search for stillness at home," first at the monastery, and then at his hermitage; his tremendous appetite for diversity in his readings, his friendships, his correspondence; and then his simultaneous urgings to "center down" into a "harmony of a unifying spirit," feverishly and enthusiastically embracing both Western and Eastern religious traditions. Further, like Siddhartha, we see Merton dealing in those tumultuous years during and after the Second Vatican Council struggling for more conversion—conversion and change not only now allowed but even encouraged by new freedoms and new interpretations (still backed up, in most part, by the "security of religious dogma").

It was John Henry Newman, many will recall, who declared that "to live is to change, and to be perfect is to change often." Himself a monk who took the Benedictine vows of stability and *conversatio*, conversion, Merton fully grasped Newman's declaration of seeking perfection by way of change and more change. His understanding of the change needed in his life was in stark contrast to the common—and humorous—change referred to in "Men's Prayer" that Canadian comedian Red Green recites half-mockingly: "Dear God, I'm a man, but I can change, I guess, if I have to."

Obviously, when we speak of conversion, we usually speak of major changes in outlooks or turnarounds. But conversion is also made up of a host of small changes in habit and practice as well. I recall being part of a group speaking some years ago with kindly Brother Raphael, then guest master at the retreat house at the Abbey of Gethsemani. Someone in the group wanted to know how far away it was to the Merton cinder-block hermitage. "This will tell you something of my former life," quipped Brother Raphael, "but it is about a par four to the front door there."

But for Merton, his former life was of a more worldly and undisciplined manner. He often drank to excess, his sexual history was checkered to say the least, having fathered a child. His life was, in the view of many and finally very much in his own view, out of control and in danger of implosion. In time, the Trappist monastery was to be the antidote.

Says Anthony Padovano in his book *A Retreat With Thomas Merton,* "Grace seems to be granted by God only when we stop living the life we have had. Merton apparently felt this way when he entered the monastery. He burned his books, terminated his doctoral study, intended never to write again, turned his back on the world, and defined as reality only that part of the planet occupied by Gethsemani, Kentucky."

In the late 1930s, Merton was angry at the world, but even more angry that he himself was part of the reason for this poor state of the world. He became a Catholic in November, 1938, because he believed that faith was one of the few real answers to a messed-up life, a messed-up world. Faith could bring order, hope, and he certainly hoped, forgiveness—albeit a life of much penance would be part of the bargain.

Later he was to learn some of the more subtle definitions of conversion. It is not all about renunciation and perfection, but about seeing the extraordinary in the ordinary; in effect, it is about becoming who we are, even if that is flawed. Yes, one must strive to be responsible and moral, but also vulnerable, trusting, spontaneous in our love for neighbor, accepting of oneself.

In *A Retreat With Thomas Merton*, Padovano says Merton had a studied response to unworthy emotions such as envy or anger or sexual temptation: They "can often be brought into line," Merton believed, "not by attacking them violently and seeking to repress them, but by making our lives emotionally richer." Padovano goes on to say that as time went on, Merton came to see that sinful temptations were the result of a diminished view of life, and emotional enrichment—a walk in the woods, enjoying poetry, music, and the arts—were far superior to self-punishment. Conversion, indeed, had changing definitions for Merton over his lifetime. The same will be true, no doubt, for us.

And for Merton, once aware, once enlightened, once educated, he knew he could no longer be neutral. He could no longer commit one of love's great enemies—the sin of indifference. There would be no more neutrality about war, arming for war, greed, political corruption, or ignorance (even or especially by the Church).

Merton on Conversion

Just why did you come to this desert? Well, I know why *I* came here: It's a *refugium peccatorum* (refuge for sinners)."—Merton mutters this under his breath as he is speaking to novices studying to join the monastery.

Without a true *metanoia*, a true conversion of one's whole life, monastic discipline is an illusion. There must be a total reorientation of our entire being from the love of self to the love of God. The monk cultivates 'contempt' for the world in the sense in which the world is opposed to God. But at the same time, he retains his love for and concern with all those souls redeemed by Christ, who are struggling to find Him and serve Him even in the midst of the world—and above all for those who, loved and sought by Christ, never think of Him and have never, perhaps heard His holy name.

I am aware of the need for constant self-revision and growth, leaving behind the renunciations of yesterday and yet in continuity with all my yesterdays. For to cling to the past is to lose my continuity with the past, since this means clinging to what is no longer there.

Distinguish this from death-wish and frustration. It is at once an acceptance of not existing any longer (whenever I shall cease to exist in this state I am in) and a full acknowledgment of the good of existence and of life. In reality, it is the acceptance of a higher, inconceivable mode of life entirely beyond our own control and volition, in which all is gift. To resign oneself to not being what one knows in order to receive a totally unknown being from a totally unknown source and in that source.

It is not complicated, to lead the spiritual life. But it is difficult. We are blind, and subject to a thousand illusions. We must expect to be making mistakes almost all the time. We must be content to fall repeatedly and to begin again to try to deny ourselves, for the love of God.

Applying Conversion to Our Lives

I have always struggled with the idea of sustainability. That is, I can be good for rather long periods of time; I can be faith-filled for long periods of time; I can even be thankful to God for all God's gifts to me for quite some lengths of time. What I cannot seem to do is sustain all these traits. It all reminds me of the great Flannery O'Connor short story "A Good Man Is Hard to Find."

O'Connor was a great Catholic author of Merton's era who was always filled with surprises. She was a very devout Catholic, and it is reported that when an interviewer challenged her faith in the Eucharist, she simply blurted out, "If it's a symbol, to hell with it!" In "A Good Man Is Hard to Find," O'Connor tells of a family ambushed out in the country by some thugs, including a character called "the Misfit." As it ends up, the Misfit takes the grandmother out and actually shoots her, killing her.

Afterward he tells his gang about the grandmother, saying, "She would of been a good woman if it had been somebody there to shoot her every minute of her life." Quite an indictment. (One reviewer said that Flannery O'Connor's stories leave a nasty taste in your mouth. I can understand that. But they are worth it!) But there is a moral to her story: Do we need a gun constantly held on us to be good, to be nice, to be, for that matter, truly *converted*?

For Reflection

It is wise for all of us to keep the phrase "Always we begin again" in mind. The point is that we, as people, change—and we keep changing. Look at Merton's change from rebellious young adult to docile novice to devout young priest to confident author and spokesperson to challenger and changer of some beliefs and practices both public and private that had stood firm for ages.

Merton, through it all, was mindful that this change, these workings, were the workings *of* God and *for* God. Michael Mott's outstanding biography, *The Seven Mountains of Thomas Merton*, details this especially well, tracing the various stages of Merton's revised views and attitudes toward God, monasticism, politics, civil rights, peace, the Church, and the very responsibilities of monks as well as all Christians alike.

As to our own conversion, the cliché is that some one-time trip to a "sweat lodge" or retreat or youth camp or seminar or spiritual fitness program of one type or another will do the trick for us. In the 1930s there were "think houses" built by the wealthy. These were places of retreat, places where one could think through matters of concern. Any or all of these can make a dramatic difference. But, as Merton knew, it is really the new habits and practices performed every day, large and small, that make conversion possible. We are coming to know that we can't just go on some new diet or perform some new and magical exercise that will make us physically fit. Rather, we must change our very lifestyles, adopting improved personal habits, and thereby become "new and improved."

Merton, we "born Catholics" remember, was a convert. His upbringing had been mostly devoid of formal religion, and his conversion from unbeliever to believer was not an overnight occurrence, where he suddenly sat bolt upright in bed with the answer. Merton knew that sort of thing happened mostly in the movies, in the trenches during the heat of battle, behind bars as the parole hearing approached.

Merton's conversion was the kind that was genuine and the kind that stuck—gradual, studied, accumulative. No doubt his final decision seemed sudden to many, but it was the result of a long and pain-filled process of searching and not finding. And then, once baptized into the Catholic Church, he was enlightened to the fact that this believing thing, this conversion, had to be nurtured, strengthened, renewed, and sustained at the price of ongoing sacrifice and dutiful practice. The frying pan—and the fire—were to do this forging. Gethsemani had both.

What do *we* have? It is different for each of us. But it is the pearl of great price.

CHAPTER FOUR

Single-Heartedness

What matters is not spirituality, not religion, not perfection, not success or failure or this or that, but simply God, and freedom in His Spirit. All the rest is pure stupidity.

Contrary to the title of this chapter, the thing many of us like best about Merton is that he was a perpetual seeker; he was forever, ceaselessly, unendingly, searching. The search just never seemed to end, and we can all relate to that, no matter how blessed we are. With Merton, as we see in reading his journals especially, his search only began once he chose to become a Catholic Christian. First he wanted to become a Franciscan, only to enter the Trappist Abbey of Gethsemani instead.

Soon enough his Gethsemani honeymoon was over and he was puzzling over becoming a Carthusian instead, or being sent off perhaps to a new foundation in Utah, or a mission on a

Mexican island. Then it was the Camaldolese that tempted him; then the idea of a simple hermitage, in which he did live for three years; but then this became too busy what with all the visitors and distractions; so he puzzled long and hard over the possibility of something even more remote: perhaps a faraway hermitage in Alaska…or New Mexico…or California…or in Asia? Farther and farther into the desert his mind wandered. And it was never to be alone with himself, but to seek God more earnestly.

Here is a sample of his thinking as early as 1947: "I don't care. God is guiding me. He wants me in solitude, in poverty and alone with Him. Every time the smoke clears, the first thing I am conscious of is the Holy Ghost saying, 'No, this way! Be quiet! Get off in a corner and forget things and set your house at rest and wait.'"

Note, however, that this chapter is about single-heartedness, not single-mindedness. Merton's mind was filled with ideas; it was a mind that was always searching, looking around, evaluating, exploring, restless. His head, as is true of creative, learned intellectuals, was brimming with a multitude of ideas. But it is always clear that his heart was set on only one thing: to be a monk and thereby please God in his every thought and action.

His way of life was not normal; he was a monk. Embracing celibate chastity and voluntary poverty, the monk finds security and fulfillment in God alone. He obeys his superior as

Christ, and he values prayer as the first priority. He values work as service to honor God by loving others, and he does this rooted in one place (stability) for life. These are the essential elements of monasticism. Thus the monk is different. But then all Christians are called to be different according to their particular vocations: to be like Christ, "a sign of contradiction" to the popular culture surrounding us.

The Desert Mystics (third and fourth centuries), then St. Benedict (fifth century), and St. Bernard of Clairvaux (twelfth century), all laid the foundation for the life of constancy that was the life of a Trappist monk in Merton's day, and our day today. What they did, and do, is weave God into the very cloth of everyday life. One is never far from God, and God is never far from us.

The entire daily and nightly program of official prayer times is called the "Hours" or the "Divine Office." And, interestingly, the short midday prayer services are called the "Little Hours." Why? Because they are short. And yet they are essential in order to keep God constantly in one's mind and heart. Sometimes people wonder whether this fixed schedule takes the spontaneity out of prayer, but the answer is that this "practice, practice, practice" instills the habit of prayer and contemplation. If our days are fully punctuated with a regimen of practice times it is very hard not to be making progress toward a life of single-heartedness.

Everyone who came to know Merton has said he had a terrific sense of humor and a great laugh. But they also say he was a very serious guy. If you listen to any of the recorded talks he gave to Gethsemani novices in the 1960s, you immediately pick up both: humor and seriousness. As to his no-nonsense side, he often, in his talks and in his writings as well, came off as rather dogmatic; the word "must" comes up often, as do such phrases as, "There is no doubt…"; "I can say with certainty…"; "It is perfectly clear that…." Merton, in other words, was not only himself convinced and convincing in his convictions, he wanted others to be as well. He was all about evangelization and rallying God's people to the same single-heartedness he possessed.

There is an old saying that we should trust those who seek the truth—and doubt those who say they have found it. Merton was a seeker, and this, if anything, is what he teaches anyone who observes him or reads his words or studies his extraordinary life.

Merton's friend, a fellow Trappist in the community and his confessor, Fr. Matthew Kelty, preached a sermon in the 1980s that came to be an article called "Wild Geese." In this sermon he proclaims that "There is no beauty without the harsh dedication to the common, to the love of Jesus with one another and for a dying world that so needs the witness of men who believe what they say." It is from this same Merton comrade,

Matthew Kelty, that we find words that express the purity and single-heartedness of a kindred spirit in prayer. This dramatic creed is from Kelty's book *Flute Solo*. I recorded it in longhand in 1985, and still today I have not read anything quite like it:

> He will never leave me, not really. And in the empti-
> ness which is solitude, in the wild night of the barren
> desert, he cannot hide from me. And even if the sun
> should never rise and the night be without end, I will
> still believe, even if I wait for all eternity. Though he
> never answer, I will yet knock, and knock again. He
> fools me not; I am wise to him. I know him. I know
> he loves me, so I do not care what he does. And in life
> without care, what joy of heart.

And so it was that Merton—and Kelty, and the rest of their Trappist community—*believed* what they sang in the monastic choir all those many years: The monks on one side of choir stalls sing at Compline, "And you shall not fear the terror of the night…" and the other side saying in their hearts, "You got that right, brothers," and with their voices, "nor the arrow that flies by day…."

And hundreds and thousands of monks over the ages have done the same, singing the same psalms, expressing their singular love for God there in the monastic choir and in their very rising and reclining, in their living and praying, their working and their going to bed, resting in their conviction that "Even at night I go to bed and sleep comes at once for you alone, Lord, make me dwell in safety."

Merton on Single-Heartedness

Even if everything else goes…provided you have your Faith, and are united with others in Faith in a Christian community of some sort, you have everything. Nothing can take it away. Nothing can take away what you are. You have to develop it yourself with God's grace. What you have to work at is your prayer…. What you have to do is simple. It centers around Faith. Develop your Faith.

I have never for a moment questioned the vocation to be a monk, but I have had to settle many other questions about ways and means, the where and the how of being a monk.

Maybe this time it is the end. I hope I have stopped asking questions. Have begged her for the grace to finish the course here and die as a holy monk in the monastery or in solitude closely dependent on the monastery. I feel great peace and my heart has never been so free, so poor and so empty.

In the monastery everything has to be justified because everything is very seriously under question. Here only I am under question, and it is right for me to face the doubt which is my own empirical self, myself as question, knowing that in myself I also have Christ as answer.

> There is one thing more—I may be interested in Oriental religions, etc., but there can be no obscuring the essential difference—this personal communion with Christ at the center and the heart of all reality, as a source of grace and life.

Being Single-Hearted in Our Lives

Are you one of those lucky and much-blest persons who have everything one could possibly want, and yet…? I remember a time when I was a young adult and I was driving my cool, new car down the road, on my way to pick up my wonderful girlfriend, listening to my favorite music, a nice drink in my cup holder. I loved my girlfriend and she loved me; I loved my job and my life. And yet I thought to myself, looking around in the car, "What's missing? This is crazy!"

Not an uncommon feeling, of course. And what was missing, as the brilliant St. Augustine concluded many centuries earlier, was that I was still a human being. And by our nature, we humans must struggle, as Augustine noted when he addressed God in one of his most famous lines, "You have made us for Yourself and our heart is restless until it rests in You." Interestingly, Thomas Merton has been called "the modern-day St. Augustine": human, restless, one who experienced a radical conversion from his former ways.

For Reflection

Thomas Merton's monastic life was nothing less than a feat of single-heartedness. Distracted as we are by complicated lives, are we able to hand over our lives in trust to the God whom Merton sought his entire life to love and serve?

We may never be as dramatically drawn into spiritual reality as Merton was, and our response may be far less wholehearted than Merton's. But it is clear we are all called to renounce whatever it is that is in the way of our relationship with God. It might be good to name the things that detract or distract us from the wholeness and holiness of what God has created.

Nothing about losing our life is easy. The mainstream culture we live in makes demands on us that are hard to resist, and our integrity can be easily compromised. What will it take to find the strength to become more single-hearted despite cultural pressures to the contrary?

We will find that there are big ways—and little ways—to speak up, to take a stand, to express our convictions on behalf of living and spreading the Good News, as Merton did. Fr. Matthew Kelty lived well into his nineties. In his later years, he liked to tell the story of himself speaking up at an abbot's council meeting at Gethsemani. One early spring he recommended that the abbey use one of the tall and skinny farm siloes as a Christian symbol. Easter was approaching and he suggested an artist come and weld a bright steel "flame" of sorts on top of the silo, and paint down the side, "Alleluia!" Says Kelty, "My recommendation didn't even make the minutes of the meeting."

In another way, though, Kelty knew—as did Merton—that the monk or hermit's lack of "practical usefulness" is what gave the life its special freedom. When the poet W.H. Auden wrote in his poem "In Memory of W.B. Yeats," that "poetry makes nothing happen," he wasn't complaining; he was rejoicing.

CHAPTER FIVE

Prayer and Contemplation

In prayer we discover what we already have. You start where you are and you deepen what you already have and you realize that you are already there. We already have everything, but we don't know it and we don't experience it.

It seems an understatement, and rather trite to say it, but Merton believed in the power of prayer. He believed, along with thousands if not millions of others, that prayer can bring benefits of healing, transformation, grace, conversion, and perhaps even freedom from want itself. He firmly believed, as do many, that when individuals pray, when families and communities pray, God answers those prayers in a loving manner. On numerous occasions he expresses the sentiment that if it were not for the fervent prayers of whole communities—like the Trappists, the Franciscans, large communities of sisters and brothers and priests, and small ones as well—the world would slip off into the realm of darkness and despair and ruin.

Thomas Merton may have obsessed about many things, but there is one, single theme that he spent the greatest portion of his life studying and practicing and writing and speaking about. That was the contemplative life, and contemplation itself. We try to make the case in this book that there was a bare minimum of fifteen themes that mattered greatly to Merton, themes such as humility, pleasing God, nonviolence, and so on. But many would go so far as to say that it was thanks to Merton, more than any other individual in modern times, that everyday people had and have discovered contemplation as a rich means of spiritual advancement.

Contemplation is no easy matter, not even after every detail and circumstance has been arranged for this purpose. I am speaking of the monastery now, the place with all the right ingredients for a life of prayer and contemplation. Shortly after Merton entered the monastery he was in for a disappointing realization about the purity of his prayer life and his motives. The monks knew, after all, that having an arsenal of pre-rehearsed spiritual notions in one's head was a real plus when life got tough. Habits of daily psalm verses, spiritual reading, repeated hymns, daily Mass, and regular reception of the sacraments all filled that valuable arsenal.

Picture the scene: Prayers uttered in repetition, chorused by a hundred male voices on a winter night with the big abbey church an echo chamber, all of it resembling the principle of the Tibetan prayer wheel, that prayer repeated enough at some point becomes something unspecified and miraculous. And it does. Thoughts and habits change, participants become fortified, and it becomes second nature to draw from these wellsprings in times of need. When something goes wrong, the first thought for the well-practiced is perhaps a prayer such as "Lord, have mercy," rather than the more common curse or condemnation that the rest of us might utter without any thought.

In Merton's recollection of his early days in the monastery, he recounts that he had the flu and was confined to the infirmary. For him, the infirmary was anything but a hindrance to his life of prayer; it was, as a matter of fact, a blessing to be there, giving him every opportunity to pray, to do what he wanted to without having to run all over the place in response to the bells that were constantly calling community members to their next appointment at prayer or work. He felt like a child having an unexpected day off from school.

But he has an awakening moment at some point; he is suddenly forced to recognize that this self-centered attitude reveals that all of his bad habits had sneaked into the monastery with him: as he named them, spiritual gluttony, spiritual sensuality, and spiritual pride. In other words, it was all about him, Thomas Merton, and his own individual need for satisfaction.

Merton made the humbling admission that he needed to correct his attitude and motivation: His goal was not to attain some dramatic, private religious experience that would make him feel both happy and secure. No, he mustn't allow himself to have his own private, feel-good religious experience. Rather, his prayer and contemplation need to be other-directed, God-directed, an experience of communion with God and others—an experience removed from the realm of acquiring something for oneself, but, instead, a moving toward an unselfish giving of something to God and other human beings.

In a letter he wrote to Sufi scholar Ch. Abdul Aziz, Merton described his method of contemplation: "It is not 'thinking about' anything, but a direct seeking of the face of the invisible, which cannot be found unless we become lost in him who is invisible."

Merton goes deeper in the prayer he composed, his "Prayer to Our Lady of Mt. Carmel": "Teach me to go to the country beyond words and beyond names." He realized in his later years especially that contemplation was about self-emptying and freedom from self-awareness. This was the path to an infinite relationship with God.

We make the whole thing too complicated, he keeps implying:

> It's a risky thing to pray, and the danger is that our very prayers get between God and us. The great thing in prayer is not to pray, but to go directly to God.

If saying your prayers is an obstacle to prayer, cut it out. Let Jesus pray. Thank God Jesus is praying. Forget yourself. Enter into the prayer of Jesus. Let him pray in you. (The Jesus Prayer is the best way to forget that you are praying. But don't take away from weak people the crutches they need.)

The best way to pray is: stop. Let prayer pray within you, whether you know it or not. This means a deep awareness of our true inner identity. It implies a life of faith but also of doubt. You can't have faith without doubt. Doubt and faith are two sides of the same thing. Faith will grow out of doubt, the real doubt. We don't pray right because we evade doubt. And we evade it by regularity and by activism. It is in these two ways that we create a false identity, and these are also the two ways by which we justify the self-perpetuation of our institutions.... But the point is that we need not justify ourselves.

Merton scholar Jonathan Montaldo says that in the end, in Merton's last year of 1968, Merton was not trying to figure out how he could become more socially active. Rather, he was looking for more and more solitude. This was always upper-most in his consciousness. And the silence was not about peace and quiet and rest and comfort, it was about environment—a "place" where he could go deeper and deeper into experiences of prayer and meditation that would transform his consciousness.

Merton had written in his journals, "I need something that I don't even know yet, something that I don't even know that I don't have." "And that's what he was looking for on his Asian trip," says Montaldo. "He wasn't going to hit the streets. He wasn't going to get married. He was going to go into deeper meditation."

Merton on Prayer and Contemplation

So it is with one who has vanished into God by pure contemplation. God alone is left. He is the "I" who acts there. He is the one Who loves and knows and rejoices.

Meditation is a twofold discipline that has a twofold function. First it is supposed to give you sufficient control over your mind and memory and will to enable you to recollect yourself and withdraw from exterior things and the business and activities and thoughts and concerns of temporal existence, and second—this is the real end of meditation—it teaches you how to become aware of the presence of God; and most of all it aims at brining you to a state of almost constant loving attention to God, and dependence on Him.

As a man is, so he prays. We make ourselves what we are by the way we address God. The man who never prays is one who has tried to run away from himself because he has run away from God. But unreal though he be, he is more real than the man who prays to God with a false and lying heart.

People who try to pray and meditate above their proper level, who are too eager to reach what they believe to be 'a high degree of prayer,' get away from the truth and from reality.... We do not want to be beginners. But let us be convinced of the fact that we will never be anything else but beginners, all our life!

However, the important thing is not to live for contemplation but to live for God. That is obvious, because, after all, that is the contemplative vocation.

Learning to Pray and Be Contemplative in Our Lives
I had the benefit of being taught by members of a community of Benedictine nuns as a child in elementary school. They were truly pious and devout individuals to whom I remain grateful. But when it came to prayer and all things leading to holiness, they took things pretty far. For example, as I look back at my eight- or ten-year-old self, I feel that the sisters made prayer and holiness a competition. They tried to make little prayer machines out of us. And we good-heartedly tried to fall in line.

I remember my cousin, who was in my same grade, boasting as we walked to morning Mass that he was making every step he took a prayer. Trying to top him, I replied that I was making every hair on my head a prayer. He then one-upped me by saying he was making every step he took ten million prayers.... You get the idea.

And then there was the matter of martyrdom. It was the 1950s and the godless Communists were all around, it was feared. We had been reading the lives of the saints about this time, all about martyrs who would subject themselves to all kinds of tortures and even death rather than say yes when asked if they would abandon their faith in God. It was a scary time for us kids.

Our more mature faith now tells us that we are indeed to become martyrs—day after day after day. Not necessarily dying, but making one sacrifice after another in order to feed the hungry, clothe the naked, and visit the sick, imprisoned, and lonely. It's all in Matthew 25, the Last Judgment parable, and just as powerfully in Jesus's questioning of Peter. Peter assures Jesus of his love for him three times, each time more emphatically, when Jesus asks, "Do you love me?" Christ's simple reply each time is, "Feed my sheep."

This is how we are to show our love for Christ, then, by feeding the hungry, literally and figuratively. Prayer and devotion are essential, but even more important is the love of God in our prayer and the love of neighbor in our everyday actions.

For Reflection

Do we take prayer more seriously than God does? In *Seeds of Contemplation,* Merton talks about prayer and our human weaknesses and foibles. For one thing, he notes that distractions are part and parcel of prayer, and not to be abhorred. Indeed, prayer is not to be a perfect experience. We are human beings and are intended to be human, and that means flawed. That does not mean our lives are not sacred and we cannot be holy.

Reflecting on all of this, author Anthony Padovano relates in his book *A Retreat With Thomas Merton:* "I have had no more unsettling experience in pastoral work than the confession by most people that they have lived inadequate lives, that they are not worthy and good, that God will not be easy with them because they have made so many mistakes."

Indeed, for all of this, again it is Merton who is such a wondrous example of one who wants to pray well and sometimes does, who wants to please God and sometimes does— and sometimes does not. Padovano, in the same text referred to above, concludes the discussion with a question as Thomas Merton himself might have done: "Do you tend to take prayer more seriously than God?"

CHAPTER SIX

Nonviolence

You cannot claim to be 'for Christ' and espouse a political cause that implies callous indifference to the needs of millions of human beings and even cooperate in their destruction.

A pacifist by nature, as early as October 1935, when Merton was twenty, he joined the local Columbia University peace movement. This was triggered by Italy's daring invasion of Ethiopia. As part of his enrollment in the movement, he took the Oxford Pledge to not support any government that undertook war.

Merton balanced his passionate views with an analytical realism, however, later saying that overwork and activism can actually destroy our peacemaking efforts, and that in our busyness to do everything and have so many projects going on we are actually succumbing to violence. Quite a profound irony.

He also was proud that his voice was being taken seriously on the subject of nonviolence. In October of 1961, he wrote, "it appears that I am one of the few Catholic priests in the country who has come out unequivocally for a completely intransigent fight for the abolition of war and the use of nonviolent means to settle international conflicts. Hence by implication not only against the bomb, against nuclear testing, against Polaris submarines, but against all violence."

And Jesuit Fr. John Dear (himself nominated several times for the Nobel Peace Prize, most notably by Archbishop Desmond Tutu in 2010) was one of his greatest admirers in this area of singling out individuals who have made an historical difference: "I submit that we'll never really know the deep influence of Merton on all of us. Today in the Catholic peace movement in the United States, anyone who is serious about working to stop war and nuclear weapons and the direction the country is going in has learned the lesson of Thomas Merton: that this work is so hard, and that we're in for such a long haul, that it's got to begin with contemplative prayer. Merton taught us all that, and we're learning that lesson. And that's different from where the peace movement was in the 1960s. I hope we've matured or we're deepening, so that we're not just angry activists. We are spiritual people who are trying to move toward the God of peace as Merton called us to, as Merton did."

As to civil rights, he was to say, accusingly, that this was not a black problem, but a white problem. For Merton, reflecting on one's self is part and parcel of nonviolence. Martin Luther King, Jr., said that unless people were convinced history was on the side of justice they ought to leave the civil rights movement. Merton might have gone so far as to say unless people were convinced that God was on the side of justice, the same is true.

God, indeed, is on the side of unity—and violence violates unity because it separates human beings. Merton believed that we could not hurt another without ultimately hurting ourselves. Conversely, we cannot help another without ultimately helping ourselves.

Kathleen Deignan has been long involved in peacemaking efforts through interreligious dialogue. She describes Merton's stance as "the Jesus tradition of nonviolence," and strongly asserts that Merton had this unrelenting commitment. She states that, "It's very, very difficult for the Christian tradition to really honor the extreme nonviolence of Jesus and find its home in the world at the same time. I think, within the Christian tradition, we have made our agreements or compromises with what we call reality. Merton didn't go there. Although I think he was a realist, he stayed very much on the side of this prophetic witness of Jesus and the early gospel tradition, to the way of nonviolence, to the celebration of life at all cost, within an empire of death."

One can examine almost any of Merton's writings on racism, poverty, injustice, and find the incredible relevance of his words for our times, even though they were written in the 1950s and 1960s. And his words encourage all involved in this "Jesus tradition of nonviolence" that our lives are not ineffective if we do not see much fruit from our efforts. Merton assured all who would read or listen that lives devoted to peace and justice will bear great fruit, because God is using these efforts in ways we could never see.

Merton on Nonviolence

I am against war, against violence, against violent revolution, for peaceful settlement of differences, for nonviolent but nevertheless radical changes. Change is needed, and violence will not really change anything: at most it will only transfer power from one set of bull-headed authorities to another. If I say these things, it is not because I am more interested in politics than in the Gospel. I am not. But today more than ever the Gospel commitment has political implications....

Why...is there so much hatred and so dreadful a need for explosive violence? Because of the impotency and the frustration of a society that sees itself involved in difficulties which, though this may not consciously be admitted, promise to be insuperable. Actually, there is no reason why they should be insuperable, but as long as white society persists in clinging to its present condition and to its own image of itself as the only acceptable reality, then the problem will remain without reasonable solution, and there will inevitably be violence. The problem is this: If the Negro [sic]… enters wholly into white society, then *that society is going to be radically changed.*

Those who have invented and developed atomic bombs, thermonuclear bombs, missiles; who have planned the strategy of the next war; who have evaluated the various possibilities of using bacterial and chemical agents: these are not the crazy people, they are the sane people. The ones who cooly (sic) estimate how many millions of victims can be considered expendable in a nuclear war, I presume they do all right with the Rorschach ink blots, too. On the other hand, you will probably find that the pacifists and the ban-the-bomb people are, quite seriously, just as we read in *Time*, a little crazy.

Today I realize with urgency the absolute seriousness of my need to study and practice nonviolence. Hitherto I have "liked" non-violence as an idea. I have "approved" it, looked with benignity upon it, praised it even with earnestly…. I need to set myself to the study of non-violence, with thoroughness. The complete, integral practice of it in community life. Eventually teaching it to others by word and example. Short of this, the monastic life will remain a mockery in my life. It will extend to civil disobedience where necessary. Certainly to non-cooperation in evil, in monastic politics. But polite, charitable, restrained.

Being Nonviolent in Our Lives

It is November 23, 1985, and I am at Gethsemani, reading a rare book by Trappist Fr. Matthew Kelty called *Flute Solo*. He wrote it while a hermit in Papua New Guinea. His reference to the necessity for social action hits me between the eyes: "My point is that the world itself is a desert today. No one has to become a monk to enter it. But like the monk we ought as Christians to respond to the scene not with a program but with a faith that can stand in the midst of chaos and firmly believe that back of it all is a loving God."

Pope Francis has galvanized many people today with his bold proclamations that as Christians we must be about social action, a natural extension of loving our neighbor, more than about doctrine and rules. This is what Jesus taught, and Merton clung tenaciously to this teaching especially through his efforts in the area of peace and nonviolence in the later years of his life.

He was often ostracized by the hierarchy for his beliefs, but like Gandhi, Merton believed that we could not be true to our God-given humanity without a dedication to nonviolent means of resolving conflicts.

For Reflection

Hannah Arendt wrote in 1969 that "The practice of violence, like all action, changes the world, but the most probable change is a more violent world."

Merton was fully behind the notion of activism to promote peace, justice, and nonviolence, but even more so he was behind God's fidelity to humanity, and our need to accept this as the ultimate way to a more just and peaceful world:

> Hence I must forget my bitterness and love His fidelity, in compassion and concern for all who are, without knowing it, gall and bitterness in His world that His joy may change us all and awaken us to His truth. And that we may live His truth in fidelity and eliminate injustice and violence from the earth. If we seek this at any rate, He will live in us. The results are not in our hands.

What does the concept of nonviolence mean to you? Can you make its practice as an integral part of your life?

CHAPTER SEVEN

Humility and Being Human

When humility delivers a man from attachment to his own works and his own reputation, he discovers that perfect joy is possible only when we have completely forgotten ourselves. It is only then that we pay no more attention to our own deeds and our own reputation and our own excellence that we are at last completely free to serve God in perfection for His own sake alone.

There is plenty of self-reproach in the Merton journals. But, indeed, there is an even greater abundance of genuine humility.

Legend has it that Merton was once confronted by a complete stranger in Louisville, when there for a medical visit, and was asked, "Aren't you Thomas Merton, the famous writer?" Merton replied simply, "Actually, I'm a Nelson County farmer" —which he was, of course, among other things.

For most of his adult life—especially after the unprecedented success of *The Seven Storey Mountain*—Merton had to fight the attractions of ambition and celebrity. He had become so famous that he could have called his own shots if he lived out in the world. Within the monastic community, his vow of obedience made it a different story, one he was willing to abide. He knew in his heart that his gifts were from God, and that his renunciation of the world included the renunciation of fame and fortune.

Merton wrote in *The Silent Life:* "In order to be free with the freedom of the children of God, the monk gives up his own will, his power to own property, his love of ease and comfort. His pride, his right to raise a family, his freedom to dispose of his time as he pleases, to go where he likes and to live according to his own judgment. He lives alone, poor, and in silence. Why? Because of what he believes."

With his national and even international celebrity after 1948, Merton had a world of options at his disposal. His publishing friend, James Laughlin of New Directions, was involved in the publication of twelve of Merton's books. He came to know Merton well, and would sometimes hear him complaining about life at the monastery. Laughlin says he once challenged Merton with the statement and question: "you're a brilliant writer, you could go out in the world. You could still do your spiritual teaching, you'd be a very successful writer. Why do you stay there?" Laughlin says Merton looked at him incredulously and said, "You don't understand. That's where I belong.

That's my home." Indeed, it was the only home he really had in his lifetime.

Something similar happened in 1967 when the famous folk singer Joan Baez, with her friend Ira Sandperl, came to visit Merton. After a picnic and a drink or two, Ira started pushing Merton with a question: "Why don't you just go to Bangkok?" Merton replied, "Well, that's a good idea but you don't understand this life. You take vows, and one of the vows is you do as you're told to do." Baez goes on to conclude about Merton that "he was a strange combination—he was this good, obedient monk, and he was a rebel, a rebel as a Church person. And I imagine that man tucked so far away but speaking so forthrightly gave priests and nuns and other Church people the courage to take steps they otherwise wouldn't have taken."

Merton on Humility and Being Human

In all these things I see one central option for me: to let go of all that seems to suggest getting somewhere, being someone, having a name and a voice, following a policy and directing people in "my" ways. What matters is love…. Monday is my 51st birthday. Hence the summing up.

And it is only when we pay no more attention to our own deeds and our own reputation and our own excellence that we are at last completely free to serve God in perfection for His own sake alone.

Humility consists in being precisely the person you actually are before God; and since no two people are alike, if you have the humility to be yourself, you will not be like anyone else in the whole universe.

To be little, to be nothing, to rejoice in your imperfections, to be glad that you are not worthy of attention, that you are of no account in the universe. This is the only liberation. The only way to true solitude.

So pure is the joy of being man that those whose Christian understanding is weak may even take this to be the joy of being something other than man— an angel or something. But God did not become an angel. He became *man*.

Being Humble in Our Lives

Fr. Jeremy King, a Benedictine monk friend and former classmate of mine at Saint Meinrad, likes to tell one story of Thomas Merton's humility and complete lack of personal celebrity. Back in the early 1960s, when Merton was novice master at the Abbey of Gethsemani, there was a young man aspiring to become a Trappist monk. He therefore attended all the novice conferences given by Merton. After a year or so, the young man had discerned that he did not have a vocation to become a monk, and left Gethsemani.

It is only years later that he finds out that his novice director had been the famous Thomas Merton. At the monastery, Merton was "Father Louis," but also at the time the conditions at Gethsemani were so restricted and restrained (no talk, no newspapers, radio, TV, etc., especially for novices) that Merton's celebrated status out in the secular world was unknown to many at the abbey.

For Reflection

St. Bernard of Clairvaux, an early founder of the Cistercians, had a clear perspective on how the virtue of humility was to be lived. He was known to tell his community members, "Love to be unknown." He also wrote: "It is not enough to be subject to God, unless you are subject also to every human creature for the sake of God.... If then you wish to be perfect in righteousness, make the first step towards him who is less than you; defer to your inferior, show respect to your junior."

What does this mean for us, as people out in the world? It means being very forgiving—particularly, forgiving others for not being God! We human beings want and need so much, and when we expect all of this from our spouses or our children or our brothers and sisters, we are bound to be disappointed time and again. So we have to keep on forgiving. And, just as important, we have to seek forgiveness for our own faults. That is the secret to humility.

Another secret to humility is uncertainty, as Pope Francis has spoken about so eloquently and with such lack of inhibition:

> If a person says that he met God with total certainty and is not touched by a margin of uncertainty, then that is not good. For me, this is an important key. If one has the answers to all the questions—that is proof that God is not with him. It means that he is a false prophet using religion for himself. The great leaders of the people of God, like Moses, have always left room for doubt. You must leave room for the Lord, not for our certainties; we must be humble. Uncertainty is in every true discernment that is open to finding confirmation in spiritual consolation.

CHAPTER EIGHT

Pleasing God

I am happy that I can at least want to love God.

Merton came by it honestly—pleasing God, that is. He had fully absorbed the Holy Rule of St. Benedict, and one of its most significant tenets: "Let us prefer nothing to the love of Christ." This continues as one of the major mottos of the Benedictine life. Cistercians—Trappists—follow this same Holy Rule of St. Benedict, but with stricter observance. And yet for Merton, after his personal spiritual conversion, it seemed to come naturally to want to please God; he did not need to look it up or read about it in a book of holy rules.

Once Merton was accepted into the Order at Gethsemani in 1941, he came to debate a central question about himself as a writer: Did his writing please and honor God or did Merton write for his own benefit or fame or self-satisfaction? This was a question he was still debating almost to the end of his life. Was this, his major life work, something God desired of him? He was to struggle with this mightily.

In many ways, his writing talents were his strongest suit, even though the occupation of writer could fill up one's days—and nights—with a multitude of concerns about topics, accuracy, quality, style, suitability for publication, censorship, pleasing his agent and editors, delays in response from his publishers. Add to this the halo of celebrity it placed upon him: He was deemed an expert beyond what he believed was warranted; he was constantly bombarded with questions and requests from friends, professionals, and complete strangers.

And so he suffered through many occasions of confusion and worry, all the while knowing his writing could perhaps make more difference in a troubled, hungry-for-God world than anything else perhaps, except his prayers and the prayers of his community of monks.

His most familiar, most famous, and most loved of prayer is all about pleasing God and getting past the confusion and worry we all experience in finding ways to do so:

> My Lord God, I have no idea where I am going, I do not see the road ahead of me, I cannot know for certain where it will end. Nor do I really know myself, and the fact that I think I am following your will does not mean that I am actually doing so. But I believe

that the desire to please you does in fact please you. And I hope I have that desire in all that I am doing. I hope that I will never do anything apart from that desire. And I know that if I do this you will lead me by the right road, though I may know nothing about it. Therefore I will trust you always though I may seem to be lost and in the shadow of death. I will not fear, for you are ever with me, and you will never leave me to face my perils alone.

Throughout his monastic years, he kept moving inward, as we can see, always reassessing his priorities, reexamining the rightness and fit of it all. He was one, clearly, who would agree that when it came to setting priorities, urgency and necessity could set a new agenda. He was one, for example, who would clearly have agreed with the great Holocaust survivor and writer Elie Weisel that, to paraphrase, when you see someone suffering and it is not you, it is more important that you think about that person and what you can do to help him or her, than to think about God.

Merton's times, just as our times, called for this kind of ongoing examination of just what it was that would most please God. Merton constantly adapted to this, as you can especially see in his journals where he keeps making notes about what he wants to keep on the front burner and what he feels may need to be shoved toward the back.

As late as the end of 1965, Merton was still writing in his journals on the topic of pleasing God. He wanted this to be the central motivation for everything he did: "Therefore, clear necessity for *one* task above all now: collection and direction of inner strength upon what I know of God's will, to let it move me completely, and to move with it. (If there is any confusion of motives this is *impossible*.)"

Merton on Pleasing God

Each one of us has some kind of vocation. We are called by God to share in His life and in His Kingdom. Each one of us is called to a special place in the Kingdom. If we find that place we will be happy. If we do not find it, we can never be completely happy. For each one of us, there is only one thing necessary: to fulfill our own destiny, according to God's will, to be what God wants us to be.

It is terrible to want to belong entirely to God, and see nothing around you but the world, and not see Him. In the monastery you don't see Him either, but you have nothing to do but lament your separation from Him, and to pray to Him, and pray for the world.

I have found myself a pretty good cross. Question: just because a cross is a cross, is it the one God wants for you?... Just because it is obedience, does that make it meritorious? Pleasing to God? I wonder. I don't ask these questions in a spirit of rebellion; I would really like to know.

It seems to me the most absurd thing in the world to be upset because I am weak and distracted and blind and constantly make mistakes! What else do I expect! Does God love me any less because I can't make myself a saint by my own power and in my own way? He loves me more because I am so clumsy and helpless without Him—and underneath what I am He sees me as I will one day be by His pure gift and that please Him—and therefore it pleases me and I attend to His great love which is my joy.

Last night it snowed again. The sky looks like lead. It is about as dark as my own mind. I see nothing, I understand nothing. I am sorry for complaining and making a disturbance. All I want is to please God and to do his will.

Pleasing God in Our Lives

In the middle of my career, I was offered an attractive new position in top management. I was to be the director of all publications and products produced by our sizeable company. In my heart it did not seem a great fit, as I have always been one to desire a fairly narrow focus on which I could concentrate my efforts fully.

And yet I knew this new position held a great deal of influence over what we created and produced—and hand in hand with that, the potential for great influence on the spiritual lives of our tens of thousands of customers. In short, to me it looked and smelled and tasted like God's will. I genuinely thought this was a call from God to do something bigger for the kingdom. I don't think I did it for the money.

Well, it may have been God's will, and it may not have been for the money, but after two laborious and troubling years I was begging to go back to my old job. And when I finally got that old job back, I knew that was where I belonged, and where God would help me succeed. I was back to my prayer of gratitude: "Thank you God; I feel I was made for this!"

In the late 1950s, the superiors of Merton's order were seriously considering whether or not to grant him a transfer to a more remote location. He had desired a location of more privacy and quiet (preferably a hermitage, as we know), for a long period of time. What the new possibility offered was some degree of this perhaps, as he was to live and work at a mission on a small island off Mexico.

Wrote Merton in his journals: "More and more the only thing that makes sense is to take the Mexico project not because

I like it, but because so far it seems to be the most likely to be the Will of God. Not because it seems likely to succeed—but because I think in my heart that I can please God by attempting it. Not dropping it seems likely to fail. Staying with it for the love of God and purely for that alone."

Merton, as we know, ended up not making the change. But it does show his genuine willingness to do what he thought would please God. This was always uppermost in his mind.

For Reflection

Most of us operate on the level of wishing God would please us by fulfilling all of our desires. Ralph Waldo Emerson, in a tongue-in-cheek fashion, once quipped, "A great man is coming to eat at my house. I do not wish to please him; I wish that he would wish to please me."

What would we want more if God were to come to our house—to please God or to have God please us?

CHAPTER NINE

Silence and Solitude

Spectacular view. Wide-open spaces. No cable.

Merton once made the observation that our silence is shattered not by our speaking but by our eagerness to be heard by others. We do want to be heard, and Merton wanted to be heard as well.

Now that I have been visiting the Abbey of Gethsemani every year since 1981, I tell people that there, you can hear everything—and you can hear nothing. It is the quietest place on the face of the earth. By contrast, I lived and worked for a combined thirty years at Saint Meinrad Archabbey, a Benedictine monastery and seminary in southern Indiana. Saint Meinrad is a very quiet place also, but not like Gethsemani, which is even more rural.

At Gethsemani, what is most noticeable is that there is very limited conversation between monks and guests. With that comes the distinct feeling of barrenness and austerity. This was and is, after all, a community of Cistercians of the Strict Observance, where silence *is* observed. And even though there were some 240 monks and candidates residing at Gethsemani when Merton entered the Order, silence was one of the hallmarks of the institution.

The writer Thomas Mann said, "Solitude gives birth to the original in us, to beauty unfamiliar and perilous—to poetry."

The truth is that Merton saw himself as a writer. He affirmed this early on:

> It is possible to doubt whether I have become a monk (a doubt I have to live with)," he states early in his monastic career, "but it is not possible to doubt that I am a writer, that I was born one and will most probably die as one. Disconcerting, disedifying as it is, this seems to be my lot and my vocation. It is what God has given me in order that I might give it back to Him. In religious terms, this is simply a matter of accepting life, and everything in life as a gift, and clinging to none of it, as far as you are able. You give some of it to others, if you can.

But to be a writer, at least a writer who could produce the tremendous volume of quality works Merton produced, simply requires a great deal of solitude and discipline. These endless days and hours of solitude can be quite perilous as they may take the writer far, far into the depths. At the same time it may also give one an intense appreciation for spells of deliverance from the writer's cell. We see this again and again over the years with Merton, the sometimes-taciturn writer/solo artist reaching out in friendship, both for professional interaction as well as sheer companionship. He, the lonesome hermit-writer, had hundreds and hundreds of friends.

Behind all of this, it is most interesting to note that the word *paradise* comes from the Old Persian word, *pairidaeza*, meaning "a walled space." The definition gives no indication of the size of such a walled space. For Merton, the size kept getting smaller. His paradise for so many years was the walled space of the big monastery, the cloister ("Go to your cell and your cell will teach you everything," was the ancient wisdom from the early monastics and desert elders.) In his later years the only thing big about his idea of a paradise was that it would open out onto the great expanses of nature.

And yet, Benedictine Sr. Suzanne Zuercher says it was actually more complex than that. She writes in *Merton: An Enneagram Profile,* "Rather than withdrawing into a narcissistic self-concern and self-protection, Merton plunged himself into his monastic community, where the need to balance solitude and solidarity led to a kind of desert he had not anticipated."

Even in his later years, says Zuercher, Merton never quite

succeeded in living completely the life of a hermit; his superior and brother monks would never allow that, insisting instead that he join them for some meals, weekly conferences, and so on. In this way they perhaps saved him from the trap of role-playing the solitary, the hermit and kept Merton's feet on the ground.

Concludes Zuercher: "His later public recognition and lessened monastic restrictions about socializing also brought him back to center. He began to live more of what most of us would call a 'normal life' in his last years." It was at this stage in his life that people felt they came to know "the real Merton," because now he was a bit more free—and more vulnerable as well—in his maturity. Even then, as we find in his journals, his most difficult struggles were private ones. And these he was to work at in silence and solitude.

Despite being a people person—making everyone he met feel very special and unique in his or her own right—Merton was, if anything a gregarious recluse. Visitors were a constant issue with him, and he sometimes did not want to change the situation. He knew that he himself was a big part of these "socializing" problems. And so time and again he made fervent vows to do better, to be more discerning, less social—more serious, perhaps even to the point of excluding almost everyone. After all, as he wrote in his journal, as late as June 15, 1966: "For me solitude is not a problem but a vocation."

Merton on Silence and Solitude

There should be at least a room, or some corner where no one will find you and disturb you or notice you. You should be able to untether yourself from the world and set yourself free, loosing all the fine strings and strands of tension that bind you, by sight, by sound, by thought, to the presence of other men.

If you seek escape for its own sake and run away from the world only because it is (as it must be) intensely unpleasant, you will not find peace and you will not find solitude. If you seek solitude merely because it is what you prefer, you will never escape from the world and its selfishness; you will never have the interior freedom that will keep you really alone.

I went to bed late at the hermitage. All quiet. No lights at Boone's or Newton's. Cold. Lay in bed realizing what I was: I was *happy!*

My life is a listening, His (God's) is a speaking. My salvation is to hear and respond. For this, my life must be silent.... If our life is poured out in useless words, we will never hear anything, will never become anything.

The truest solitude is not something outside you, not an absence of men or of sound around you; it is an abyss opening up in the center of your own soul.

Applying Silence and Solitude to Our Lives

In my early years in the religious publishing world, we published a wonderful little book called *An Accidental Monk*, by Marylee Mitcham. I remember one of the great lines from her book: "Someone recently came up to me and asked me what I was doing. 'I am *practicing being content*,' I replied." The author was the mother of a young family, trying to live, with her husband and children, the simple life—a quiet, peaceful, holy life. She told her story well, and her line about practicing contentment has stuck with me.

As to solitude, it occurred to me some years ago to perhaps start up a new journal. I would call it *The Solitude Journal*. I told one of my business associates my idea and she quickly responded, "You might be the solitary subscriber!" Maybe, but Thomas Merton could have brought it off beautifully.

Another experience of peace and quiet and silence comes to my mind. My wife and I went to nearby Bloomington, Indiana, several years ago when the Dalai Lama was giving a talk at a church there. There were also a good number of religious dignitaries joining in the event, and they sat up near the altar with the Dalai Lama.

After a powerful talk and some inspiring music, we were asked to participate in a period of silent meditation. It was to be for thirty minutes. Well, most of the folks in attendance were agreeable to this. In the church's balcony, however, there were the media people with their cameras—lots of cameras.

Click-click-click it went for the full thirty minutes. *Flash-flash-flash.* The silence and solitude with God was simply interrupted, much to our chagrin.

The one thing all this clicking and flashing commotion demonstrated is how important silence is for contemplation. More and more in our loud and fast world, silence demands solitude. As difficult as it may be to make time for silence it is essential to maintain a healthy spiritual life and sense of self.

Solitude can be intimidating, especially if you are the type of person who thrives on activity. Yet Merton would stress that even for activists, there is a need for an imaginary hermitage into which you can retreat; you don't need a physical hermitage. One's contemplative side must be both cherished and nourished. He pushed this idea in his extensive correspondence with the Berrigan brothers, Daniel and Philip, who were leading peace activists at the time.

Merton compared an activist without an inner contemplative side to a dragon chasing its own tail and then chewing on it. There is always the danger of acting for the sake of activity rather than acting for any good. Merton's message was that one had to go up to the mountain, like Jesus, and spend time in prayer and recollection. Then you are prepared to come down from the mountain and reengage in the activity that builds up the kingdom.

For Reflection

Who of us today can go to one's room—or "cloister"—and be content? Who can spend a Sunday afternoon doing mostly nothing? Who even knows what the word *saunter* means anymore? Who wants to wait for anything—especially to wait in silence?

When it comes to media, most of us want to be not only informed by the media, not only entertained; we want to be impressed by the dazzle and drama and the flash. As to sporting events, we do not do so well with baseball; too many lulls in the action. Basketball? Actually, just show us the last shot at the buzzer in overtime. You tell your child to turn off the video game and go outside to play and he says, "What is this—1962?!"

Thomas Merton knew the importance of peace and quiet, of silence and solitude. Early on in his monastic life within the community, Merton was reading and researching the lives of the hermits of old. He discovered at the very least that inner solitude, detachment—a hermitage of the heart—were the minimum requirements for serious prayer and meditation. As he saw the modern world getting louder, more crowded, more demanding, he saw the need for a little cloister of his own. But even his hermitage had become less than ideal (partly due to his own need for social contact).

On one leg of the last trip he would take, in India on November 18, 1968, he wrote, thinking of Gethsemani: "Though I fully appreciate the advantages of the hermitage at Gethsemani, I still have the feeling that the lack of quiet—and the general turbulence there (external and internal) last summer are indications that I ought to move." Though just a few sentences later he notes, "It (Gethsemani) is my monastery and being away has helped me see it in perspective and love it more."

He gave utmost importance, despite everything, to the solitude and the silence. We require these in our lives as well, to assure time and space to ponder eternal questions. These things are necessary for us in order to take the "narrow way" Jesus asks us to take, the way Thomas Merton took.

Where can you find a place in your life for silence and for solitude?

CHAPTER TEN

Work

We don't need so much to talk about God but to allow people to feel how God lives within us, that's our work.

Ora et labora—prayer and work—are at the foundation of every Western monk's life. The *labora*—work—part has had various interpretations and manifestations depending on the time or era one lived in. In the early days, up to not very long ago, manual labor was essential simply for the very survival of the monastery. Thus, farming, cooking, baking, weaving, shoe-making and so on were a necessary part of every monk's day.

In later times, monks were better educated than the masses of society, and thus their work had larger ramifications. Activities such as educational and missionary work were deemed appropriate. The latter was true for Merton, albeit he did his fair share of manual labor willingly and earnestly, even though it is often recounted that he was a tad clumsy and nonmechanical.

In his time, farming was the major enterprise of the abbey, followed by the cheese making and fruitcake baking work that supports the monastery today. (We shouldn't forget the delectable bourbon fudge concoction also made at Gethsemani.)

Merton was assiduous about his work, whatever the time or occasion, and he fully appreciated its merits. Even in his later years when he was a student of Zen, he knew well the admonition of the Zen teaching, "After enlightenment, do the laundry." As to the nature of his work, Merton knew that his life could never be about total escape or comfort. Indeed, comfort without conscience was as bad as the power and wealth without conscience that he so intensely opposed in his work, his writings.

Merton was quite a student of and expert on St. Bernard of Clairvaux. Some of Merton's earliest assignments in the monastery were to write about the doctors of the Church, making their thoughts more accessible to the modern monk as well as to the rest of us.

In one of Merton's books on Bernard, *Thomas Merton on Saint Bernard,* Merton gives a good summary of Bernard's teachings about work (action), as well as prayer and contemplation. The tension that is always present between these two virtues was very present in Merton's mind, as we know well. Wrote Merton: "Although St. Bernard himself permitted Blessed Conrad to leave Clairvaux and live as a hermit, he ordinarily envisaged the contemplative life within the ordinary framework of the community, and it was his characteristic task to show that a deep life of contemplation was possible side by side with its varied and numerous activities."

Merton goes on to quote Bernard's strong advice to his "wavering" monk, Eugene, who was later to become a pope: "Do not give yourself entirely to activity, and do not engage in active works all the time. Keep something of your heart and time for meditation!" Merton's literary output, his major work beyond the physical duties of monastery life he had over the years, was absolutely astounding, especially considering the quality of so much of that work.

In August of 1967, he was asked to write a letter to "an ordinary person" who was inquiring about the contemplative life of a monk. Merton begins by saying that, regrettably, his letter will be a dashed-off affair. He then proceeds to write a minor masterpiece, of which he himself says, "Such are the few ideas I have had, written in haste—so much more will be said so much better by others." In my own view, the following insights provide some of the most profound and moving insights from Merton's entire literary canon. Note the sheer power, the poignance and poetry, in his conclusion of the letter:

Whether you understand or not, God loves you, saves you, and offers you an understanding and light which are like nothing you ever found in books or heard in sermons. The contemplative has nothing to tell you except to reassure you and say that if you dare to penetrate your own silence and dare to advance without fear into the solitude of your own heart, and risk the sharing of that solitude with the lonely other who seeks God through you and with you, then you will truly recover the light and capacity to understand what is beyond words and beyond explanations because it is too close to be explained: it is the intimate union in the depths of your own heart, of God's spirit and your own secret inmost self, so that you and He are in all truth One Spirit. I love you, in Christ.

Merton on Work

The most important, the most real, and lasting work of the Christian is accomplished in the depths of his own soul. It cannot be seen by anyone, even himself. It is known only to God.

If you write for God, you will reach many men and bring them joy. If you write for men, you may make some money and you may give someone a little joy, and you may make a noise in the world—for a little while. If you write only for yourself, you can read what you yourself have written, and after ten minutes you will be so disgusted you will wish that you were dead.

How weary I am of being a writer. How necessary it is for monks to work in the fields, in the rain, in the sun, in the mud, in the clay, in the wind: these are our spiritual directors and novice-masters. They form our contemplation. They instill us with virtue. They make us as stable as the land we live in. You do not get that out of a typewriter.

My spiritual life is poor here, and the "exercises" that are supposed to help one I find *stultifying*. They leaden the mind and spirit. (Except man[ual] labor.)

The Meaning of Work in Our Lives

I am grateful for the fact that during most of my life I have had the good fortune of doing work that I loved and believed in. By the same token, I recall many times feeling overly zealous, overly ambitious; I believed that the work I was doing was "anointed" work—or that was the excuse I gave for the many sacrifices my family had to make due to my absences and preoccupations and obsessions. I had read a number of times Merton's admonition that, "An activity that is based on the frenzies and impulsions of human ambition is a delusion and an obstacle to grace…. It is in the ordinary duties and labors of life that the Christian can and should develop his spiritual union with God."

And yet I found it difficult indeed to find balance, even though at the time I was working for and with the Franciscans, and then the Benedictines—both masters of simplicity and moderation! Equally ironic is that in the midst of all of this, I wrote two small books, filled with advice that I myself found so hard to take. The titles tell the story: *Slow-down Therapy* and *Keep-life-simple Therapy*. Sure.

We can't always love the work we are doing. Sometimes we must do things simply because they need to be done, like household chores or our daily routines of hygiene. You might be working just for a paycheck; as much as we'd all like to have jobs in which we are passionate about what we are doing, it's not always possible, especially in the difficult economy of today's world.

But what we can do is undertake our tasks, our work, with a sense of higher purpose, knowing that this is the necessary "stuff" of living, of being human. Merton would be the first to affirm this.

For Reflection

> I have been absurdly burdened since the beginning of the year with the illusions of "great responsibility" and of a task to be done. Actually whatever work is to be done is God's work and not mine and I will not help matters, only hinder them, by too much care.

Can we try adopting this attitude? Can we find joy in whatever task is at hand, to the best of our ability, knowing that this is in the service of our Creator?

CHAPTER ELEVEN

Now

There is no question that I really feel I am living a saner and better life. I would not exchange this for anything even though for four days a snake was living in the jakes. (I finally persuaded him to go elsewhere I hope!) In spite of the hornets, the noise of machines in the fields, the dogs and hunters, etc. All this is plain ordinary reality without any need of ideology or explanation. It *is*. That is enough.

As the years went by, Merton came to be much preoccupied with questions about peace, war, and nonviolence. The year 1962 shows much attention to these matters. And yet, at the same time, he was happily reawakening to nature and the wonder of the particular moment: rainstorms, snowflakes, cornfields, the song and flight of birds. He comments widely in his journals, expressing awe, celebration, thanksgiving, and praise. There is little doubt this helped him immensely in his ability to be less critical of society, community, everyday life, and more accepting of God's plan. He was clearly becoming more and more accepting of mystery on many levels.

Merton took his life seriously—perhaps too seriously sometimes, as even he would have to agree. But he wanted to live life intentionally, with purpose, with care, with direction, with intensity, and awareness. This can drive one crazy. And even though he fought this inner drive or drivenness, Merton was constantly combating the urge to be *doing*. He found it a challenge to keep things in balance—especially when it came to the active versus the contemplative life, doing versus being.

In many ways it is overstimulation that keeps us from enjoying now. This was also true, at times, for Merton. Some cynics would say he had too much time on his hands. But indeed he was spending a great deal of his time scheming, planning, making little promises to himself about changing this or that. This was to be his pattern year after year, for many a year. And it was only when he grew older that he began to practice more of what he preached—including slowing down and living in the now.

Merton on Now

> To go out to walk slowly in the woods—this is a more important and significant means to understanding, at the moment, than a lot of analysis and a lot of reporting on things "of the spirit."

How absolutely true, and how central a truth, that we are purely and simply part of nature, though we are the part which recognizes God.

The rain ceases, and a bird's clear song suddenly announces the difference between heaven and hell.

Made more coffee. From the silence of the valley I can learn that certain questions do not need answers of mine, or not now.... Wait! Do nothing yourself. You will see.

If therefore we seek Jesus, the word, we must be able to see Him in the created things around us—in the hills, the fields, the flowers, the birds and animals that he has created, in the sky and the trees. We must be able to see Him in nature. Nature is no obstacle to our contact with Him, if we know how to use it.

Being in the Now of Our Lives

I made a note in my journal years ago, which I often did at Gethsemani, after the evening reflections offered by Fr. Matthew Kelty following Compline. "A monk makes a quiet investment in wonder," he said. The monk is not compelled to create wonder but humbly to receive it, he further explained. All of us are called to do the same.

One of the things Thomas Merton and I have in common is the same Enneagram number, the same personality profile as designated by the Enneagram. Of the nine personality profiles that exist, according to the Enneagram, Merton was a number 4; I share this number. For those of you unfamiliar with this profile, people who are 4s, as the terminology goes, have tendencies toward being melancholic, over-dramatizing, romantic, and artistic. In 1996, Suzanne Zuercher, O.S.B., wrote a wonderful book called *Merton—An Enneagram Profile,* and in it she talks about the strengths and weaknesses of folks with this profile, specifically of Merton:

> Hope is born out of despair. Despair comes to us when all the avenues of possibility and plan have been explored and are dead-ends. For 4s, script writers and organizers of the future by instinct, despair is accompanied by an additional dimension; it tells them that what they do best fails them in the long run. The future cannot be controlled, and that future includes relationships, work, and ultimately sickness and death. There is only the present moment, 4s come to realize, and it is a realization that leaves them feeling trapped and enslaved. No longer can the now be made more interesting and energizing and possible by embellishing it with future fantasies. Eventually 4s must face that there is nothing to do but face the

moment. No longer can they delude themselves by looking back at what was or forward at what might be. There is only the straightforward—and therefore the contemplative—encounter with the only life any of us has: life in the present.

Pretty heavy—and perhaps dramatic in itself, all this. But the Enneagram and Zuercher's analysis of Merton's personality profile are truly instructive and revealing, even while exploring darker dimensions of given personalities. Zuercher quickly counters what may seem as harsh with the brighter side: "We must not forget…the other side of the coin of this 4 instinct. How Merton discovered his compulsions, made peace with them, and let them lead him down the path of humility…. His grappling with, giving up on, eventually turning over to God… are reasons we remember him today. These dynamics are why he brings us comfort and speaks to our pain."

For Reflection

One does not need to be a 4 on the Enneagram, obviously, to be in the habit of living too much in the past or in the future, versus the present. All humans are to some degree fretful of what will come of their lives, the lives of their children, their jobs, their health. They are worried about their car, their furnace, or their lungs, all making funny noises. Or we spend a lot of time regretting what we did or did not do, what was said, the decisions we made, the sadness and hardship we've encountered thus far.

Not to be facetious, but one response is to "consider the lilies of the field," as Jesus put it in Matthew 6:28. Or "consider the trees," as Merton comments so many times in his journals. Trees, for one thing, are stable; they aren't going anywhere. Merton says that the sound of the breeze blowing through the pine trees is better than any prayer he can compose; he says that a walk in the woods brings delight that begins to overpower him from head to toe. Their majesty and beauty offer him a peace that smiles in the very marrow of his bones.

Here is one of my favorite Merton quotes. It is actually a prayer in which he is waxing poetic. These beautiful, inspiring lines concentrate on the present moment and generate a sense of true freedom from cares:

> The trees, indeed, love you without knowing you. The tiger lilies and corn flowers are there, proclaiming that they love you, without being aware of your presence. The beautiful dark clouds ride slowly across the sky, musing on you, like children who do not know what they are dreaming of, as they play. But in the midst of them all, I know you, and I know of your presence. In them and in me I know of the love which they do not know, and, what is greater, I am abashed by the presence of your love in me.

CHAPTER TWELVE

Unity and Community

My heart breaks with need of vision and help for the world.

Merton would never have had that mystical experience in Asia near the end of his life had it not been for his keen and sensitive sense of ecumenism. It was at Polonnaruwa where he looked at the giant sleeping Buddha statues in all of their tranquility that he was "jerked clean out of the habitual, half-tried vision of things…and all life is charged with dharmakaya…everything is emptiness and everything is compassion." It was truly a unifying vision, similar to the unifying vision at Walnut and Fourth Streets in Louisville, Kentucky, much earlier in his life, where he saw that all his brothers and sisters were one in life and in God's love.

His monastery placed an almost extreme emphasis on a group form of community living, as it does today to a great extent.

Community, for one thing, makes us strong; it makes (or allows) us to do things we would never do on our own. For example: Get up at 3:15 and praise the Lord at *Lauds*; raise up a building where we gather to pray. Or, as one wise and holy person put it: "How else are you going to wash somebody else's feet?"

For Merton, there were a lot of feet to wash—both inside the monastery and out in the world—via his extraordinarily large community of correspondents and his extraordinarily large reading public. Inside the monastery, he had kindred spirits as well with whom he could share values and do intellectual sparring. And despite his call to solitude, Merton became more and more concerned with making connections between the monastery and the wider world.

One day while in Louisville, he had a mystical experience in which he seemed to "wake from a dream of separateness" from the rest of humanity. He began to see clearly that his vocation could not be one of escape from the world but a life of compassion and integration and solidarity with others.

In the 1960s, a substantial portion of Merton's work, his thoughts and writings, contained more than just overtones of that Haight-Ashbury era, but a real sense of East meeting West, of cosmic oneness. Wayne Simsic, in his book *Praying with Thomas Merton*, tells us that by 1964, Merton was suggesting that the contemplative life must not close monks to the outside world but should make each monk even more sensitive to the needs of the time. Simsic continues to explain Merton's view: "Monks should learn to empathize with the suffering of other people. Just as all Christians need to serve humankind, so monks must also. They serve by praying, by providing islands of retreat, and by witnessing silently that life is more than power and possessions. In Merton's case, he served his sisters and brothers by writing books and articles that challenged injustice and violence and by mentoring the many people who asked his guidance."

Merton on Unity and Community

The lives of all are inextricably mixed together, and the salvation and damnation of souls is involved in this inescapable communication of freedoms. Either we will love and help one another or we will hate and attack one another, in which latter case we will all be one another's hell.

There is only one true flight from the world: it is not an escape from conflict, anguish and suffering, but the flight from disunity and separation, to unity and peace in the love of other men.

The unutterable confusion of those who think that God is a mental object and that to love 'God alone' is to exclude all other objects to concentrate on this one! Fatal. Yet that is why so many misunderstand the meaning of contemplation and solitude, and condemn it.

Whatever I may have written, I think it can all be reduced in the end to this one root truth: That God calls human persons to union with Himself with one another in Christ.

The deepest level of communication is not communication, but communion.... It is beyond words... beyond concept. Not that we discover a new unity. We discover an older unity. My dear brothers (and sisters), we are already one. But we imagine that we are not. And what we have to recover is our original unity. What we have to be is what we are.

Finding Unity and Community in Our Lives

I wrote the following on a postcard from Gethsemani to my wife about ten years ago while on retreat there. On the picture side of the postcard is a photograph of the monastic community in choir. Here is my poem:

To My Spouse
The monks
On the other side of life
Are another side of me.

While they sing
Of God alone,
I sing
Of God
And thee alone with me.

Even as a hermit, Merton would join his community at Gethsemani as needed. His other great community was his many readers and correspondents, a connection that kept him grounded and that abated the danger of becoming too isolated in his own thoughts and teaching.

For Reflection

Community, for Merton, meant his brothers at the abbey, but also the world community, the Church. Merton was sensitive to the needs of all his brothers and sisters all over the world, and he states his feelings most strongly in the book *Life and Holiness*: "Of what use is it to hold seminars on the doctrine of the Mystical Body and on sacred liturgy, if one is completely unconcerned with the suffering, destitution, sickness, and untimely death of millions…? What are we doing…?"

As I write this, Pope Francis has expressed the same sentiment in an interview, talking about how we, the people of the Church, are to be like members of a field hospital, bandaging wounds, administering healing help to all who are suffering from injury, disease, poverty, and distress. Only then, after these healing ministrations, should we be thinking about the deep aspects of theology or doctrine. "The will of Christ is above all that we love one another," says Merton, and Pope Francis echoes this today.

Who are the people who keep you grounded, and who reflect God for you?

CHAPTER THIRTEEN

Honesty

A good loneliness, a good insecurity. Stone room,
pines. His will, His mercy. An imperfection to say it,
and to insist: lack of faith. Do not explain.

Talk about honesty. Here is a guy—Merton—whose most
famous prayer begins with the words, "My Lord God, I have
no idea where I am going."

Merton was a person who was unrelentingly honest with
himself. He was always digging deeper and deeper for the truth,
what was real and genuine and honest. He spoke the truth with
courage—and with love. If he ever failed on the love part, he
invariably tried to make up for it with a follow-up note or
letter or conversation.

For indeed, he did sometimes offend; he offended by his
honesty, and readily admitted that he dreaded "the politics of
permission." Says his compatriot Matthew Kelty: "He could

be tough as any one.... He could be flippant and airy, but he could also freeze you with his intensity and ardor.... He loved the monastery, yet was critical of its foibles and foolishness. He would argue and plead with his abbot the way a shrewd lawyer would argue for a lost cause, yet he was obedient to the core of his being. His obedience was tested time and time again and found pure." Kelty concludes (this written on the day after Merton's burial): "I cannot go on. You do not get this kind of person from the hands of God very often."

At the end of 1965, there was a certain amount of controversy in the air at Gethsemani because Merton was pushing to the limits his involvement in the peace movement. James Forest, of the Fellowship of Reconciliation, arranged for a retreat of peacemakers at the Abbey of Gethsemani. During the week, many in attendance were growing in frustration that their efforts seemed to be going nowhere. "We wanted to do something more serious," relates Jim Forest, "something that mattered. And Merton would say, 'It *does* matter what you're doing. If you stick to the truth and the decency of the thing, it matters. It may not have immediate, visible effect but it isn't wasted.'"

In those early years of the Vietnam War, Merton was asked many times why he didn't go out into the world and make things (peace) happen—in other words, "What are you doing inside a monastery when there are so many crises going on out here?" He responded by writing in an essay, "The only place you can stop the war in Vietnam is to be where you belong, where God wants you to be. If I give up where God wants me to be, I can do nothing....This is where God wants me to be."

As most of us know, it is sometimes a lot easier to be hypocritical than honest. Honesty, after all, can get us into trouble, as Merton himself came to find out on numerous occasions. He was not one to suffer fools lightly. And yet much of his harshest criticism is contained in his journals, where he could be most honest—and also where he could decree that they not be published until many years after his own death (and probably the deaths of many he criticized). One rather amusing if wickedly honest example:

> Dom (Abbot) James in chapter today, has highest praise for those who simply "run with the herd" (his own words), do not think for themselves, conform (he regrets that "conformism" is regarded as a bad trait by those who seek only "liberty" to "do their own will.") And he wonders why he has problems with monks leaving! And I am supposed to give a magic talk at the Abbot's meeting, to dissect the mind of youth, show where all their trouble comes from. I honestly think he expects me to say, in some way, that it all comes from radicals and self-will which is the only answer he is prepared to receive.

Merton was always testing the honesty of his thoughts and decisions, small and large. The one decision that many recall is his affair with "M," a nurse at the Louisville hospital where he was being treated in the mid-1960s. His journals for that period tell the story, and admit to the avalanche of difficulties he brought upon himself. Merton remained chaste throughout, according to most sources, although some of his passionate journal entries make for wide speculation.

On June 15, 1966, after the romantic engagement has been broken off by mutual agreement, his journal entries give his assessment of his indiscretion: "I feel once again that I am all *here*. I have finally returned to my place and to my work, and beginning again to be who I am." And just the day before his journal states: "I am better and freer in solitude, total and accepted, including loneliness and sorrow for M.—I am much more separated from everyone else, alien to the community. Very alone in the field. Invisible. 'Like a rolling stone' (Bob Dylan). M., my darling, where are you? The abbot's secretary averts his eyes in embarrassment when we meet. The gatehouse brothers smile much too politely. I am known as a monk in love with a woman."

And then with a clear, marked sense of closure, on June 19, 1966, he writes again with great humility and sincerity, mixed with more than a tincture of apology: "Who is like unto God? The secret of knowing that there is none like Him and of disposing my whole thought and being in accordance with this secret. The long labor of getting back to this center."

Merton on Honesty

My ideas are always changing, always moving around one center, always seeing the center from somewhere else. I will always be accused of inconsistencies—and will no longer be there to hear the accusation.

Sometimes I seem to be so wrong that it is frightening— yet there is always the realization that the apparently "right" course would in some mysterious way be even more wrong. And I cannot explain it. The only solution is, in all dread and humility, to accept not to be "right," and leave the consequences in God's hands.

Shall I look at the past as if it were something to analyze and think about?...as I sit in this lonely and quiet place I suppose I am the same person as the eighteen year old.... I regret most my lack of love, my selfishness and glibness (covering a deep shyness and need of love) with girls who, after all, did love me I think, for a time. My great fault was my inability really to believe it, and my efforts to get complete assurance and perfect fulfillment.

Being Honest in Our Lives

Karl Marx had cynically said that history repeats itself first as tragedy and then as farce. From the journals of Merton, and from my own journal-keeping over some forty years now, I can decidedly see that we human beings are creatures of habit. Our past frequently is an accurate predictor of our future—but not always.

For we can change, and we must. Thomas Merton, in all of his honesty, kept trying to change himself, the life of monasticism that he and many led, the very way the Church operated and some of the things it preached. Merton, again in his honesty, wanted to do something about what he saw as weak or false in anything—including himself. And the most critical thing to notice, I believe, is that he never abandoned monasticism, the priesthood, the Church, his faith, his own search for holiness, or his desire to help others along the way to holiness.

We can learn a lot from this about fidelity, despite all the mediocrity we may encounter in our world and in ourselves. We can, like Merton, seek to speak "the truth in love." We can strive, as St. Paul urges (Ephesians 4:22–23), to "put away your former way of life, your old self, corrupt and deluded by its lusts, and to be renewed in the spirit of your minds, and to clothe yourselves with the new self, created according to the likeness of God in true righteousness and holiness."

For Reflection

When have you honestly felt happiest, the closest to God, the most filled with love and joy? For Merton,

> The profoundest and happiest times of my life have been in and around Gethsemani—and also some of the most terrible. But mostly the happy moments were in the woods and the fields, alone, with the sky and the sun—and up here at the hermitage. And with the novices…. But the deepest happiness has always been when I was alone.

Take some time to recall a time or place in your life where you were perfectly content. What made this place or event so meaningful for you?

Think of a time you challenged an idea or a belief. What kept you from holding your tongue?

Think of an experience of failure in your life. Was there some element of dishonesty in the experience, on your own part or that of another?

CHAPTER
FOURTEEN

Mystery

I do not necessarily ask for clarity, a plain way, but only
to go according to your love, to follow your mercy, to
trust in your mercy.

In addition to the above statement of Merton's pure trust in
mystery, trust in love and mercy, there are two other journal
entries from the 1960s that I find most revealing and inspiring.
On August 6, 1960, he writes in *Turning Toward the World,* "The
way that opens up to me really depends on no man, not even
on myself—except that I have to leave it. And I will. For the rest
it is God's way." And then on June 30, 1966, still in the midst of
his troubling and confusing relationship with M., he seems to
wish ever so deeply to be free of the need to know what will
happen next: "Blessed are the pure in heart who leave everything to God now as they did before they ever existed."

But for many, Thomas Merton's mystical experiences help
define the man. The first was in downtown Louisville in

March of 1958. He first describes this experience in his book *Conjectures of a Guilty Bystander*. It is on the streets of Louisville, Kentucky, less than an hour from his Gethsemani home, that he realizes Christ became a human being, not a monk. Throngs of shoppers are streaming by and he suddenly has this revelation that all of these people belong to him and he belongs to them. He feels as if he were waking from a dream, finally realizing he is no better or different than his brothers and sisters everywhere. He is no longer special or chosen or separate. He awakens to the notion that it is not given only for a select few to know God; that the glory of human life is not in the things that differentiate us but in the things that unite us. To paraphrase his new understanding: If we people could only see ourselves as we are, we would kneel and worship each other!

His other most noteworthy mystical experience is the one he experiences in the East, at Polonnaruwa, not long before his untimely death. This is described in his *Asian Journal*, published after his death, and is described elsewhere in this book (see the chapter on Unity and Community).

Merton was a constant seeker of the truth. As Fr. Frank J. Matera has recently written, we all want assurance that what we believe is true. He says we seek a sign—any sign—to relieve us of the burden of believing. "In a word," says he, "we want to see in order to believe. But Jesus says it the other way around: we must first believe in order to see."

In other words we must accept mystery. That is why Merton says the monk doesn't become a monk in order to find God but to seek God. The monk needs, like the rest of us, to accept that God must ultimately remain a mystery to us until we reach our destiny. That is when we will experience the completeness that we desire and know is essential for our happiness. In the meantime, most of us "settle" for trying to find this completeness in another person, or in our possessions or our career or our experiences. Mystery is just too vague for us. Or is it?

What is this thing called "mystery," anyway? I like the analogy my friend Fr. David Knight, author of numerous books on Christian spirituality, uses to describe the term in his newest book, *The Nuts and Bolts of Daily Spirituality*. Knight says it is like sitting at the breakfast table very early in the morning, while it is still dark outside. You are sitting there with a family member or good friend, deep in conversation and having a pleasant time of it. All of a sudden you look around and, lo and behold, you notice the sun has risen and it is now daylight. It totally crept up on you! How could this be?

Says a character in Louise Erdrich's novel *The Painted Drum:*

> I've always had that longing, that need, to pierce through my existence. Mostly I have made my peace with never knowing." Merton, on the other hand, never quite gave up on his quest to "pierce

through" his own existence and the existence of all his sisters and brothers in Christ. He kept clinging to what he considered the heart and great mystery of his Catholicism—namely, that, despite the fact that Christianity is a religion of revelation and delivered to us in words and statements, "This obsession with doctrinal formulas, juridical order and ritual exactitude has often made people forget that the heart of Catholicism, too, is a living experience of unity in Christ which far transcends all conceptual formulations…. Catholicism is the taste and experience of eternal life.

Merton on Mystery

Things are what they are. See them in God.

I must gradually learn to hear and obey (God) directly in everything. There is an immense amount of nonsense in me, but He is wise and tolerates it for the time being. I must trust Him…and the false preoccupations will gradually be liquidated by His action in my life.

All the old desires, the deep ones, the ones that are truly mine, come back now. Desire of silence, peace, depth, light. I see I have been foolish to let myself be so influenced by the current trends, though they perhaps have their point. On the other hand, I know where my roots really are—in the mystical tradition, not in the active and anxious secular business. Not that I don't have any obligation to society.

What is serious to men is often very trivial in the sight of God. What in God might appear to us as "play" is perhaps what He Himself takes most seriously. At any rate the Lord plays and diverts Himself in the garden of His creation, and if we could let go of our own obsession with what we think is the meaning of it all, we might be able to hear His call and follow Him in His mysterious, cosmic dance.

Finding Mystery in Our Lives

Matthew Kelty says in one of his homilies:

> So we know so little about the simplest things, and we skirt God because He speaks mysteries, preaches an unknowable Gospel, makes unconscionable demands, advances a program too poetic and romantic to be taken seriously…. But not by all. A few listen. A few look. A few take heart because they ponder in silent wonder. They are blessed indeed. The Kingdom is theirs. And, of course, it will not stop there. Seeds grow.

For Reflection

Most of us were taught that only very special people, like saints (or people like Thomas Merton), could have mystical experiences; they are reserved for extraordinary people. We grew up thinking God did not interact with us—as if God, who created us in his own image, would not interact with us who share his life! But we need to be aware of God's interaction with us.

Think back and try to identify moments in your life when God, or an experience of God's action in our world, had a significant or life-changing effect on you. This could even have been something that happened over a long period of time—a relationship with a person, a course of study, a summer job, a vacation, and so on, an experience that changed your attitude, helped you make a crucial decision or response, turned on a light, brought you closer to God.

Naming these moments and experiences will help you in your awareness of God's desire to communicate with you, and God's desire for you to communicate with God. Like the analogy in this chapter of the sun rising totally unbeknownst to you while you were having breakfast, God wants to break through and shine on your life.

As the powerful Canticle of Zechariah, the *Benedictus*, has it: "By the tender mercy of our God, the dawn from on high will break upon us, to give light to those who sit in darkness and in the shadow of death, to guide our feet into the way of peace" (Luke 1:78–79).

CHAPTER FIFTEEN

Death and Eternity

Avoid all places where you do not hear the word "eternity" mentioned frequently.

Thinking of Merton's death, now some forty-five years ago, I am reminded of a scene in the Clint Eastwood movie *Unforgiven*. The character played by Gene Hackman is high up in the skeletal rafters of a house he is constructing. His enemies finally track him down, finding him up there working on the crossbeams, and shoot him fatally. As he falls to the ground Hackman's final, incredulous words are: "You can't shoot me; I'm building a house."

When Merton died in 1968, the house Merton was building wasn't finished either. But we get the impression that Merton would not have had an "unforgiving" attitude toward God for taking him in the very midst of the construction. Merton, after all, was building a very humble house, a shanty, a hermitage.

It was a hermitage of the heart. And, most significantly, in his writings and teachings he left us some very clear blueprints, all following God's beautiful design.

Maybe his work was finished; one of his friends seemed to think so. Dom Jean LeClercq, a Benedictine and medieval scholar who was attending the same conference there in Bangkok, when given the news at the conference that Merton had died, said, *"C'est magnifique!"* ("That's great, magnificent!")

As noted before, someone once labeled Gethsemani as "a training ground for death." Generally, people chuckle a bit when they first hear this, but once they have a better grasp of the place, nod their heads in understanding.

Thomas Merton had plenty of firsthand experience with death. He was, after all, an orphan at an early age, losing his mother when he was six, and then his father just before his sixteenth birthday. Additionally, there were the long periods where he anticipated his father's death, since his father was at death's door a number of times, only to recover. Then there was the tragic death in 1943 of his brother, John Paul, killed in World War II. Merton was twenty-eight at the time and he wrote a beautiful poem in memory of his brother. The poem begins, "Sweet Brother, if I do not sleep, / My eyes are flowers for your tomb."

As to the full body of his writings, there is an immense amount of material wherein he writes of death and eternity.

Obviously, these subjects are of central importance to the Christian, inextricably linking Christ's death and Resurrection to that of all the faithful—not to mention the faithful monk.

Merton never seemed to have a problem with the Church's teaching on death, eternity, the immortality of the soul, even though he seemed to question so many things. He lived as if he believed firmly that he would rise with Christ. And, as we have said, he wrote eloquently on the subject. For example, in the closing pages of *No Man Is an Island*, he writes:

> If, at the moment of our death, death comes to us as an unwelcome stranger, it will be because Christ also has always been to us an unwelcome stranger. For when death comes, Christ comes also, bringing us the everlasting life which He has bought for us by His own death. Those who love their life, therefore, frequently think about their death. Their life is full of a silence that is an anticipated victory over death.

And equally eloquent is this journal entry from December 7, 1962:

> Stop complaining and see at last that everything now leads in one direction: all the water is heading for the falls, and for my death, so that I must want all, eagerly, to be part of my ultimate and complete offering of

my whole life in His beloved will, beloved because it
is life giving and perfect. The will that raised Christ
from the dead.

On my retreats at Gethsemani over the years, I cannot tell you
how many times I heard Fr. Matthew Kelty say that, "Someday,
I hope I am able to perform one pure act of love for my God."
He said this repeatedly over the years. I know that he was referring to his final surrender to God at his death. But in reality
he knew, as did Merton, that he had already done it; when he
had signed up for Trappist monkhood, he was taking the most
extreme step a person of the world could perhaps take to show
his pure love for God. He had made the ultimate sacrifice of
already giving up his life—at least the life of the outside, secular
world.

I had a Franciscan priest friend who once told me that one
of the very main reasons he became a Franciscan was to try to
assure his own salvation. He simply believed this was one of the
main reasons he was put on earth—to walk a path that could
best lead him to salvation. He believed that the Franciscan way
of poverty, service to others, and denial of self were essential for
him. Like Merton, he knew that the exaggerated view of "self"
promoted by our American lifestyle had to be one of the first
things to go, and it had to go in a big way.

For Merton, this meant performing one pure act of love,

which was to die to himself and then to keep on dying, by joining the Trappists. He had only to "throw his hat over the fence"—a phrase made famous by President John Kennedy. In his last public speech, he quoted the Irish writer Frank O'Connor, who, as a boy would walk the countryside with his friends. When they came once to an orchard wall that seemed too high and difficult to climb, they took their hats and tossed them over the wall. Now they had no choice but to climb the wall. Kennedy noted that we need to climb the wall in order to explore the wonders on the other side.

For the Christian, the wonders on the other side will be ours after we live and die believing in the promises of Christ's death and Resurrection, living out the tenets of our faith.

We have noted many times that this humility, this death to the self, was most difficult for Merton. He had become in many ways a specimen—examined, probed, dissected, observed, judged—thanks to his fame, only to find that fame itself also brought its own defeats and small deaths his way. For example, in the book *An Infinity of Little Hours*, about the Carthusian life, one of the Carthusian candidates tells of his visit to Gethsemani. He says that he saw Merton while he was there, but "I was never a fan of his—I've always thought he should make up his mind whether he is a monk or a celebrity, in or out." But in the end, it was always Merton's faith that kept him in. He had thrown his hat over the tall Gethsemani fence many years before.

Thomas Merton is surely now exploring the magnificent wonders of the other side.

Merton on Death and Eternity

Why should I worry about losing a bodily life that I must inevitably lose anyway, as long as I possess a spiritual life and identity that cannot be lost against my desire? Why should I fear to cease to be what I am not, when I have already become something of what I am? Why should I go to great labor to possess satisfactions that cannot last an hour, and which bring misery after them, when I already own God in his eternity of joy?

How often in the last years I have thought of death. It has been present to me and I have 'understood' it, and known that I must die. Yet last night, only for a moment, in passing, and so to speak without grimness or drama, I momentarily experienced the fact that I, this self, will soon simply not exist. A flash of the 'not-thereness' of being dead. Without fear or grief, without anything. Just not there. And this I suppose is one of the first tastes of the fruits of solitude. So if the angel passed along thinking aloud, to himself, doing his business, and barely taking note of me neverthe-less. We recognized one another. And of course the other thing is my individual nature. But yet I might as well be, so firmly am I rooted in it and identified with it—with this which will cease utterly to exist, in its natural individuality.

But anyway I did not get the awful depression that I have had a couple of times at Christmas in recent years. Thank God for that! Perhaps this comes from my thinking about death that has opened out with the last days of Advent—seeing death as built into my life and accepting it in and with life (not trying to push it out of life, keep it away from contaminating a life supposedly completely other than it. Death is flowering in my life as a part and fulfillment of it—its term, its final chord).

Thinking about life and death—and how impossible it is to grasp the idea that one must die. And what to do to be ready for it! When it comes to setting my house in order I seem to have no ideas at all.

It is already a hard year, and I don't know what else is coming, but I have a feeling it is going to be hard all the way for everybody.

Facing Death and Eternity in Our Lives

I had the privilege to work with the Franciscans, at one of their publishing houses, for some fourteen years early on in my career. One of their primary tenets is to treat death as St. Francis of Assisi himself did; that is, to refer to her as "Sister Death." Living and working with Benedictine monks and nuns for more than thirty years now, I have had many opportunities to witness their genuine embrace of Benedict's entreaty to "Keep death always before your eyes."

In 1968 we had too much death before our eyes, as Merton himself said as the new year began. It was a horrific year of tragedies and deaths: Martin Luther King, Jr., in April, Bobby Kennedy in June, and then Thomas Merton in December. That September I had turned twenty-one. It was earlier that spring that I saw and heard Bobby Kennedy at a university rally. It was also the same year that I had turned my life away from God; perhaps it was because of all these tragic happenings, along with the Vietnam War raging and death shown before the nation's eyes every night on the news.

It would be three more years before my spiritual self came back to life. I attribute this to a new job in religious publishing where I was "forced" to read spiritual and theological works as an editor—works that made more and more sense to me the more I studied them. I came to see death less as something negative—why would God allow that to happen?—and more as a natural part of our humanity, not to be shunned or feared as much as embraced as our gateway to eternal life.

For Reflection

Here on our earthly journey, it seems that we, like Thomas Merton, are constantly seeking that sustainable Something, that elusive Stillpoint, the Center that Holds. We are looking for God. And yet throughout our lifetimes we feel that our God is always on the move: The moment we think we have "captured" God, the moment passes and we need to begin a new search.

At our death, the story changes; the restless searching ends; we are in the eternal embrace of our loving Creator. Oh, the joy in this new birth!

As Merton wrote in "Some Personal Notes" in 1965:

> I am called here to grow. "Death" is a critical point of growth, or transition to a new mode of being, to maturity and fruitfulness that I do not know (they are in Christ and in His Kingdom). The child in the womb does not know what will come after birth. He must be born in order to live. I am here to learn to face death as my birth.

CONCLUSION

It was November 23, 1985, and I was again at Gethsemani. But this time would be different. I would get a private tour of Thomas Merton's hermitage, with Fr. Matthew Kelty as my personal guide. Here I will quote verbatim from my journal entry for that day:

> Trappist, KY, November 23, 1985
>
> Arrived here yesterday on a sort of thanksgiving pilgrimage to stop by the fourteenth station of the cross and say Thanks, God, for Emily. One of my first visits here was on the day (March, 1982) it was confirmed that wife Mikie was pregnant after eight years of prayer and desperation. I remember standing in the rain at the fourteenth station asking God to make everything turn out all right. I didn't imagine he'd go and give us something so wonderful as little Emily.

I had read somewhere that Merton believed you could pray at the fourteenth station and fully expect God to answer your prayer. I will now always believe in the power of the thing.

2:15 PM—WOW!

Fr. Matthew Kelty just spent over an HOUR with me and he took me in my car to the Merton hermitage about a mile away and we both talked a hundred miles an hour. He thinks, I'm sure, that I'm "monk-happy" like the rest of them. (I will always remember his great line after Compline: "I know God loves me. So I don't care what he *does*.")

So—on this gorgeous afternoon I get to meet and get to know this great monk I've heard so much about. He was a Merton contemporary; they were born the same year; he was Merton's confessor at the end. He says he would welcome an interview especially on his years as a hermit in Papua New Guinea, and of course on Merton whom he is asked about A LOT. (This, by the way, is two days before Kelty's 70th birthday.)

He and I were talking a bit and I came to ask if he could tell me where the hermitage was, and he quickly replied, "You got a car?" Well, we almost got hung up on the mud and high ridges of the back road. "Look out over there," he says, "go over that way. You know how to drive country roads! Well, even if we get hung up I will go get Brother _____ and he will pull us out with a tractor." The same road Merton used to drive but in a Jeep that he never learned how to handle, says Kelty.

At the hermitage, all the curtains were drawn and, more to the dismay of Kelty than myself, he kept checking each and every one of them for a little opening to peek in. "I helped make these curtains," he remarked.

"This is the way Merton wanted it done," says he. "Sort of grim and all. He surely suffered here (a mile a minute). But see how it's just perfect? You can't see anything but nature. This was the Boone's land over here, Daniel Boone's family, but we bought it."

On the way back to the monastery I tried, like James Boswell after a session with Dr. Johnson, to memorize the words I heard and the feelings I experienced. I wanted to quickly record everything, word for word, because I felt this was one of those great gifts that most of us never receive. What an unforgettable experience for me. In parting he gave me a great monk-hug and said kindly, "Maybe I'll hear from you? God bless. I'll remember your name."

One hundred years from now, perhaps even one thousand years from now, there will be places like Gethsemani (and Saint Meinrad Archabbey, and so many others, including religious orders of men and women), where people will join in community to praise God and seek God's direction in an "exaggerated" way. "Exaggerated" is the term Matthew Kelty used many times when he tried to explain the contemplative, monastic life. He insisted that this life, really, was an art—and like all good art, it is exaggerated in order to make a point.

There are a great variety of opinions about this man, Thomas Merton, and some of them are perhaps incompatible. Was he, for example, a humble, holy man, a mystic, a prophet, a leader, an inspiring artist, a theologian, a teacher and spiritual director, a spiritual giant, a saint? Or was he a rebel, a troublemaker, a rabble-rouser, an ambitious egotist, a restless, unfaithful womanizer, a do-gooder, a controversial, unbecoming chap? He was certainly dangerously (to himself) introspective. He was (to his superiors) menacingly obsessive. He was on a mission, driven. He could not get away from trying to please God with his life. Jesus would simply not go away.

The vast majority of appraisals of Merton and his work come down on the positive side—especially from those who have examined his times and circumstances and upbringing. Indeed, it is in his works, which the generations have inherited, where we see Merton's greatness, a greatness far surpassing his human weaknesses. The things he stood for, not to mention the things he daringly took a stand for, show the nobility of his intentions and the vast richness of his contributions.

As for the rest of us—at least most of us—we simply like Thomas Merton. We like him because he is like us—only smarter, deeper, more profound, more serious, more intense. One wonders how he could sleep at night, he was so intense. But then perhaps he had more faith than most of us, as well— so much that he could abide in the psalm prayer he recited most nights: "I will both lie down and sleep in peace; for you alone, O Lord, make me lie down in safety" (Psalm 4:8).

Merton's gifts to us are many, and we recognize them anew one hundred years after his birth. Perhaps one of his greatest gifts is demonstrating to all of us that we can attain a unique unity with God and a new vision of our own lives. This is not something just for monks, for a select few, but for all Christians. He remarked: "My vocation is rare perhaps, but contemplation does not exist only within the walls of the cloister. Every man, to live a life full of significance, is called simply to know the significant interior of life and to find ultimate significance in its proper inscrutable existence, in spite of himself, in spite of the world and appearances, in the Living God."

For me it is Matthew Kelty who sums up Merton so beautifully for us:

He is a patron of all who would dearly love God, who would go deep to search for his light and beauty, who would do his Will, whatever and whenever.... It is not that Merton suffered more than most, so much as that he loved more, and more deeply. Therefore his engagement with God was more profound, his commitment more total, his abandonment more complete.... He was thus a perfect vehicle for God's work in the world: pure, empty, clean of self, and thus the medium of great good, then and still. The best way to honor him is to endeavor to follow him in love.

SOURCES

Introduction

*Merton, to me, was…*Rembert Weakland, quoted in Paul Wilkes, ed., *Merton: By Those Who Knew Him Best* (New York: Harper & Row, 1987), p. 163.

Courage comes and goes… Quoted in Robert J. Wicks, *Perspective: The Calm within the Storm* (New York: Oxford University Press, 2014), p. 133.

I am happy that… Entering the Silence: The Journals of Thomas Merton, Jonathan Montaldo, ed. (San Francisco: HarperSanFrancisco, 1996), p. 174.

The impulse to keep… Annie Dillard, quoted in Sage Cohen, *Writing the Life Poetic: An Invitation to Read and Write Poetry* (Cincinnati: Writer's Digest, 2009), p. 154.

This is not a hermitage… Thomas Merton: I Have Seen What I Was Looking For: Selected Spiritual Writings (New York: New City, 2005), p. 150.

There is an immense… Learning to Love: The Journals of Thomas Merton (San Francisco: HarperSanFranciso, 1997), p. 158.

Merton is one of… Ursula King, *Christian Mystics: The Spiritual Heart of the Christian Tradition* (New York: Simon & Schuster, 1998), p. 199.

I think that… Jonathan Montaldo, *Soul Searching: The Journey of Thomas Merton,* Morgan Atkinson, Jonathan Montaldo, eds. (Collegeville, Minn.: Liturgical, 2008), p. 183.

There is no other person… Lawrence Cunningham, quoted in *Soul Searching,* p. 183.

What's so shocking… David Tracy, quoted in quoted in *Soul Searching,* p. 187.

I want to see him… Jonathan Montaldo, quoted in *Soul Searching,* p. 185

Chapter One

I truly seek… A Search for Solitude: The Journals of Thomas Merton (San Francisco: HarperSanFrancisco, 1996), p. 293.

a kind of training ground… Quoted in Gerald Groves, *Up and Down Merton's Mountain* (St. Louise: Chalice, 1988), p. 39.

All I want… Adapted from *Run to the Mountain: The Journals of Thomas Merton* (San Francisco: HarperSanFrancisco, 1995).

But what more do I seek… Quoted in *Thomas Merton: Spiritual Master: The Essential Writings,* Lawrence S. Cunningham, ed. and intro. (Mahwah, N.J.: Paulist, 1992), pp. 181–182.

The center of America… Run to the Mountain: The Journals of Thomas Merton (San Francisco: HarperSanFrancisco, 1995), p. 333.

I mean I am really… Matthew Kelty, *Flute Solo: Reflections of a Trappist Hermit* (New York, Image, 1980).

The greatest joy… Entering the Silence: The Journals of Thomas Merton (San Francisco: HarperSanFrancisco, 1996), p. 168.

the one great purpose… T.S. Eliot, "Little Gidding," *The Four Quartets* (Orlando: Harcourt, 1943).

No. No lie… Leo Tolstoy, "Life Is a Lie," *The Complete Works of Count Tolstoy* (New York: Wiley, 1904).

It is terrible to want… Run to the Mountain, p. 357.

The is the center… Run to the Mountain, p. 333.

Give up everything… Entering the Silence, p. 307.

My beautiful dream… Entering the Silence, p. 307.

Afternoons are for nothing… Turning Toward the World: The Journals of Thomas Merton (San Francisco: HarperSanFrancisco, 1996), p. 100.

In the morning… A Search for Solitude, p.

Courage comes and goes… Wicks, p. 133.

Chapter Two

This is my life… Learning to Love, p. 7.

A foolish consistency… Ralph Waldo Emerson, *Self-Reliance: An Excerpt from Collected Essays, First Series* (Rockville, Md.: Arc Manor, 2007), p. 23.

If you are what you should be… Catherine of Siena, quoted in Stephen Charnock, *Treatise on Divine Providence* (n.p.: EEBO Editions, 2011), p. 368.

My chief concern… Quoted in Michael Mott, *The Seven Mountains of Thomas Merton* (New York: Houghton, 1984), p. 125.

And there will be… Mott, p. 200.

Love and do what you… Augustine, *Homily 7 on the First Epistle of John.*

One might say I had decided… Quoted in James Finley, *Merton's Palace of Nowhere* (Notre Dame, Ind.: Ave Maria, 2003), pp. 134–135.

ducks in a chicken coop… Seven Mountains of Thomas Merton, p. 297.

You want a hermitage… Seven Mountains of Thomas Merton, p. 297.

Trees and animals… New Seeds of Contemplation (New York: New Directions, 1961), p. 36

How do you expect… New Seeds of Contemplation, p. 100.

Many poets are not… New Seeds of Contemplation, p. 98

If we are called… No Man Is an Island (New York: Harcourt, 1955), p. 138.

Chapter Three

Give up everything… Entering the Silence, p. 11.

the restless departures… Quoted in Ralph Freedman, *Herman Hesse: Pilgrim of Crisis* (London: Jonathan Cape, 1979), p. 235.

to live is to change… John Henry Newman, "On the Development of Ideas," http://www.newmanreader.org/works/development/chapter1.html.

Grace seems to be granted… Anthony T. Padovano, *A Retreat with Thomas Merton: Becoming Who We Are* (Cincinnati: St. Anthony Messenger Press, 1996), p. 51.

can often be brought into line... Padovano, p. 59.

Just why did you... *The Contemplative Vocation* (Kansas City: Credence Cassettes, n.d.).

Without a true metanoia... *The Monastic Journey* (Peabody, Mass.: Galilee Trade, 1978), pp. 34–35.

I am aware... Quoted in Suzanne Zuercher, *Merton: An Enneagram Profile* (n.p.: Suzanne Zuercher, 2001), p. 112.

Distinguish this from... *Dancing in the Water of Life,* p. 3.

It is not complicated..., *Mornings with Thomas Merton: 120 Daily Readings,* John C. Blattner, ed. (Cincinnati: Servant, 1998), #103.

If it's a symbol... Flannery O'Connor, quoted in James Martin, S.J. "Flannery O'Connor and Walter Ciszek on the Eucharist," *America,* June 2, 2010, http://americamagazine.org/content/all-things/flannery-oconnor-and-walter-ciszek-eucharist.

She would of been... *A Good Man Is Hard to Find: Flannery O'Connor* (New Brunswick, N.J. Rutgers University Press, 1993), p. 51.

Chapter Four

What matters is not... *Dancing in the Water of Life,* p. 287.

I don't care... *Entering the Silence,* p. 124.

There is no beauty... Matthew Kelty, *The Call of Wild Geese* (Cistercian Studies 136).

He will never leave... Kelty, *Flute Solo.*

Even if everything else... *Merton's Palace of Nowhere,* p. 93.

I have never... William H. Shannon, *Something of a Rebel: Thomas Merton, His Life and Works, An Introduction* (Cincinnati: St. Anthony Messenger Press, 1997), p. 29.

Maybe this time... *Search for Solitude,* p. 26.

There is one thing more...Dancing in the Water of Life, p. 259.

You have made us for... Augustine, *Confessions,* 1:1.

poetry makes nothing... W.H. Auden, "In Memory of W.B. Yeats," http://www.poets.org/viewmedia.php/prmMID/15544.

Chapter Five

In prayer we discover... Quoted in David Steindl-Rast, "Man of Prayer," *Thomas Merton: Monk: Monastic Tribute* (Cistercian Studies Series), p. 80.

It is not 'thinking... *The Seven Storey Mountain* (San Diego: Harcourt Brace, 1948), p. 433.

Teach me to go... *Seven Mountains of Thomas Merton,* p. 528.

It's a risky thing... *Thomas Merton: Monk,* pp. 87–88.

And that's what he was... *Soul Searching, p. 171.*

So it is with one... *New Seeds of Contemplation,* pp. 286–287.

Meditation is a twofold... *New Seeds of Contemplation,* p. 217.

As a man is... *No Man Is an Island,* p. 42.

People who try to pray... *Contemplative Prayer, p. 37.*

However, the important thing... Quoted in Henri J.M. Nouwen, *Thomas Merton: Contemplative Critic* (Chicago: Triumph, 1991), p. 110.

I have had no more unsettling... Padovano, p. 54.

Chapter Six

You cannot claim... *Contemplative Critic,* p. 56.

it appears that I am...*The Seven Mountains of Thomas Merton,* p. 374.

I submit that we'll never... *Soul Searching,* pp. 145–147.

the Jesus tradition... *Soul Searching,* p. 149.

It's very, very difficult... *Soul Searching,* p. 149.

I am against war... *Contemplative Critic,* p. 56.

Why...is there so much... *Contemplative Critic,* pp. 129–130.

Those who have invented... Quoted in Edward Rice, *The Man in the Sycamore Tree: The Good Times and Hard Life of Thomas Merton* (New York: Image, 1971), p. 79.

Today I realize... *Turning Toward the World,* p. 239.

My point is that... Kelty, *Flute Solo.*

The practice of nonviolence... Hannah Arendt, quoted in the *New York Review of Books,* July 11, 2013.

Hence I must forget... *Dancing in the Water of Life,* p. 93.

Chapter Seven

When humility delivers... *New Seeds of Contemplation,* p. 58.

In order to be free... from a bookmark distributed at Gethsemani.

you're a brilliant writer... Quoted in *Merton: By Those Who Knew Him Best,* p. 12.

Why don't you just go... Quoted in *Merton: By Those Who Knew Him Best,* pp. 42–43.

In all these things... *Learning to Love, p. 13*

And it is only when... *New Seeds of Contemplation, p. 58.*

Humility consists in... Quoted in Thomas P. McDonnell, ed., *Blaze of Recognition: Through the Year with Thomas Merton: Daily Meditations* (New York: Doubleday, 1983), p. 83.

To be little, ... McDonnell, p. 127.

So pure is the joy... *Dancing in the Water of Life,* p. 280.

Love to be unknown... Quoted at http://archive.org/stream/sermonsofstberna-00bernuoft/sermonsofstberna00bernuoft_djvu.txt.

It is not enough... Quoted in Linus Mundy, *A Retreat with Benedict and Bernard: Seeking God Alone—Together* (Cincinnati: St. Anthony Messenger Press, 1998), p. 74.

If a person says... Quoted in Antonio Spadaro, S.J., "A Big Heart Open to God, *America,* September 30, 2013.

Chapter Eight

I am happy… Entering the Silence, p. 174.

My Lord God,… Contemplative Critic, p. 126.

Therefore, clear necessity… Dancing in the Water, p. 334.

Each one of us… Mornings with Thomas Merton, #112.

It is terrible… Run to the Mountain, p. 357.

I have found myself… Entering the Silence, p. 70.

It seems to me… Mornings with Thomas Merton, #100.

Last night it snowed… McDonnell, p. 45.

More and more… Search for Solitude, p. 343.

A great man… Emerson, "Self-Reliance."

Chapter Nine

Spectacular view… from a modern vocation recruitment ad

Solitude gives birth… Thomas Mann, *Death in Venice and Seven Other Stories* (New York: Vintage 2010), p. 24.

It is possible to… Quoted in Wayne Simsic, *Praying with Thomas Merton* (Winona, Minn.: St. Mary's, 1994), p. 74.

Rather than withdrawing… Zuercher, pp. 84–85.

His later public recognition… Zuercher, p. 85.

For me solitude is not… Learning to Love, p. 85.

There should be at least… New Seeds of Contemplation, p. 81.

If you seek escape… New Seeds of Contemplation, p. 87.

I went to bed late… Simsic, p. 54.

My life is a listening… Thoughts in Solitude, pp. 72, 88.

The truest solitude… New Seeds of Contemplation, p. 80.

Though I fully appreciate… The Seven Mountains of Thomas Merton, p. 553.

Chapter Ten

We don't need… Mary Luke Tobin, quoted in *Merton: By Those Who Knew Him Best,* p. 99.

Although St. Bernard… Quoted in Mundy, p. 63.

Do not give yourself entirely… Quoted in Mundy, p. 63.

Such are the few ideas… Quoted in Lawrence, p. 427.

Whether you understand or not… Monastic Journey, p. 173.

The most important… Life and Holiness (New York: Image, 1969), p. 56.

If you write for God… McDonnell, p. 107.

How weary I am… Contemplative Critic, p. 120.

My spiritual life… Turning Toward the World, p. 33.

An activity that is based… Life and Holiness, p. 87.

I have been absurdly… Turning Toward the World, p. 291.

Chapter Eleven

There is no question… Dancing in the Water of Life, p. 292.

To go out to walk slowly… Learning to Love, p. 23.

How absolutely true… Turning Toward the World, p. 312.

The rain ceases… McDonnell, p. 61.

Made more coffee… Learning to Love, p. 171.

If therefore we seek… Monastic Journey, p. 17.

Hope is born out of despair. … Zuercher, p. 138.

We must not forget… Zuercher, p. 19.

The trees, indeed, love you… McDonnell, p. 75.

Chapter Twelve

My heart breaks… Learning to Love, p. 220.

wake from a dream… Adapted from David D. Cooper, *Thomas Merton's Art of Denial: The Evolution of a Radical Humanist* (Athens, Ga.: University of Georgia Press, 2008), p. 151.

Monks should learn to… Simsic, p. 84.

The lives of all… McDonnell, p. 51.

There is only one true… McDonnell, p. 112.

The unutterable confusion… Dancing in the Water of Life, p. 200.

Whatever I may have written… Thomas Merton's Palace of Nowhere, p. 60. *The deepest level… The Asian Journal of Thomas* Merton (New York: New Directions, 1975), p. 308.

Of what use… Life and Holiness, p. 90.

Chapter Thirteen

A good loneliness… Turning Toward the World, p. 98.

My Lord God,… Contemplative Critic, p. 126.

He could be as tough… Matthew Kelty, *Sermons in a Monastery (Cistercian Studies),* p. 79.

I cannot go on… Kelty, *Sermons,* p. 79.

We wanted to do something… Quoted in *Merton: By Those Who Knew Him Best,* p. 55.

The only place you… Quoted in *Merton: By Those Who Knew Him Best,* p. 55.

Dom (Abbot) James in chapter… Dancing in the Water of Life, p. 143.

I feel once again that… Learning to Love, p. 84.

I am better and freer… Learning to Love, p. 83.

Who is like unto… Learning to Love, p. 86.

My ideas are always… Dancing in the Water of Life, p. 67.

Sometimes I seem to be… Dancing in the Water of Life, p. 79.

Shall I look at the past… Dancing in the Water of Life, p. 197.

The profoundest and happiest...

Chapter Fourteen

I do not necessarily ask... Turning Toward the World, p. 28.

The way that opens up... Turning Toward the World, p. 27.

Blessed are the pure... Quoted in *Learning to Love,* p. 92.

In a word... Frank J. Matera, *Give Us This Day,* October 15, 2012.

I've always had that longing... Louise Erdrich, *The Painted Drum* (New York: Harper, 2005), p. 118.

Things are what they are.... Learning to Love, p. 153.

I must gradually learn... Learning to Love, p. 358.

All the old desires... Learning to Love, p. 218.

What is serious... Quoted at http://datinggod.org/.

So we know so little... Matthew Kelty, *Gethsemani Homilies* (Quincy, Ill.: Franciscan Press, 2001), p. 61.

Chapter Fifteen

Avoid all places... John W. Donohue, S.J., "A Life Like Few Others," *America,* September 28, 1996, p. 22.

Sweet Brother, if I do not... Quoted in Robert Inchausti, *Thomas Merton's American Prophecy* (Albany, N.Y.: State University of New York Press, 1998), p. 34.

If, at the moment of our... No Man Is an Island, p. 263.

Stop complaining and see... Turning Toward the World, p. 281.

I was never a fan... Quoted in Nancy Klein Maguire, *An Infinity of Little Hours: Five Young Men and Their Trial of Faith in the Western World's Monastic Order* (New York: Public Affairs, 2007), p. 62.

Why should I worry about... McDonnell, p. 204.

How often in the last... Dancing in the Water of Life, pp. 173–174.

But anyway I did not... Dancing in the Water of Life, p. 327.

Thinking about life and... Learning to Love, p. 25.

It is already a hard year... Quoted in "The Hermit," Thomas Merton, *Spiritual Leaders and Thinkers,* http://www.fofweb.com/History/MainPrintPage.asp?iPin=SLTMERT12&DataType=AmericanHistory&WinType=Free.

Keep death always before... Quoted in Mark Alan Scott, *At Home with Saint Benedict: Monastery Talks* (Collegeville, Minn.: Liturgical, 2010), p. 286.

I am called here... Dancing in the Water of Life, p. 323.

Conclusion

He is a patron... Kelty, *Gethsemani Homilies,* p. 130.

BIBLIOGRAPHY

Atkinson, Morgan, and Jonathan Montaldo, eds. *Soul Searching: The Journey of Thomas Merton,* (Collegeville, Minn.: Liturgical, 2008).

Cunningham, Lawrence S., ed. and intro. *Thomas Merton: Spiritual Master: The Essential Writings,* (Mahwah, N.J.: Paulist, 1992).

Groves Gerald, *Up and Down Merton's Mountain* (St. Louise: Chalice, 1988).

Kelty, Matthew. *Flute Solo: Reflections of a Trappist Hermit* (New York, Image, 1980).
————. *Gethsemani Homilies* (Quincy, Ill.: Franciscan Press, 2001).

King, Ursula *Christian Mystics: The Spiritual Heart of the Christian Tradition* (New York: Simon & Schuster, 1998).

Merton, Thomas. *The Asian Journal of Thomas* Merton (New York: New Directions, 1975).
————. *Entering the Silence: The Journals of Thomas Merton,* Jonathan Montaldo, ed. (San Francisco: HarperSanFrancisco, 1996).
————. *Learning to Love: The Journals of Thomas Merton* (San Francisco: HarperSanFranciso, 1997).
————. *Life and Holiness* (New York: Image, 1969).
————. *New Seeds of Contemplation* (New York: New Directions, 1961).
————. *No Man Is an Island* (New York: Harcourt, 1955).
————. *Run to the Mountain: The Journals of Thomas Merton* (San Francisco: HarperSanFrancisco, 1995).
————. *The Seven Storey Mountain* (San Diego: Harcourt Brace, 1948).
————. *A Search for Solitude: The Journals of Thomas Merton* (San Francisco: HarperSanFrancisco, 1996).
————. *Thomas Merton: I Have Seen What I Was Looking For: Selected Spiritual Writings* (New York: New City, 2005).
————. *Turning Toward the World: The Journals of Thomas Merton* (San Francisco: HarperSanFrancisco, 1996).

Mott, Michael. *The Seven Mountains of Thomas Merton* (New York: Houghton, 1984).

Padovano, Anthony T. *A Retreat with Thomas Merton: Becoming Who We Are* (Cincinnati: St. Anthony Messenger Press, 1996).

Simsic, Wayne. *Praying with Thomas Merton* (Winona, Minn.: St. Mary's, 1994).

Wicks, Robert J. *Perspective: The Calm within the Storm* (New York: Oxford University Press, 2014) .

Wilkes, Paul, ed. *Merton: By Those Who Knew Him Best* (New York: Harper & Row, 1987).

Zuercher, Suzanne. *Merton: An Enneagram Profile* (n.p.: Suzanne Zuercher, 2001).